The Stones
in the Park

The Stones

in the Park

Richard Havers

•Opposite – *17 May 1967 at Olympic Studios, the Stones along with Andrew Loog Oldham (in hat) on one of the last occasions they were all together in the studio with their former manager*

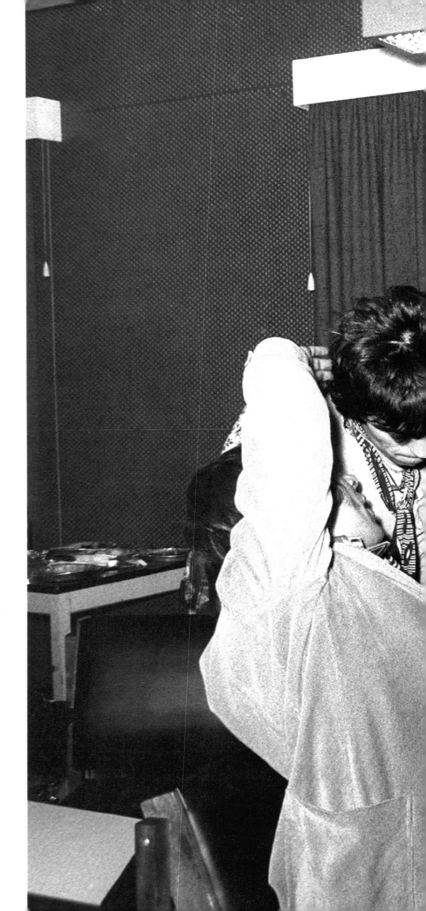

First published in 2009. A catalogue record for this book is available from the British Library

ISBN: 978-1-844258-15-4

Published by Haynes Publishing, Sparkford, Yeovil, Somerset BA22 7JJ, UK
Tel: 01963 442030 Fax: 01963 440001 Int. tel: +44 1963 442030 Int. fax: +44 1963 440001
E-mail: sales@haynes.co.uk Website: www.haynes.co.uk

Haynes North America Inc., 861 Lawrence Drive, Newbury Park, California 91320, USA

All images © Mirrorpix

Creative Director: Kevin Gardner
Packaged for Haynes by Green Umbrella Publishing

Printed and bound in the UK by J F Print Ltd., Sparkford, Somerset

Contents

THE ROLLING STONES

The Stones in the Park

For the Rolling Stones everything changed in the summer of '69. They were no longer the blues band that Brian Jones had dreamed of forming back in 1962; they had stopped being a pop band who were the ying to The Beatles' yang; and they had hardly performed on stage during the previous two years – and it was live that the Stones always excelled. Perhaps most crucially, this, was why they had lost much of their drive, which had always been at the heart and soul of all they did.

There were many other reasons behind their impasse. The drug busts, the squabbles over women, their own success that had made them the No. 2 band around the world after The Beatles – though of course for many they were and will always be No. 1. But beyond their own lives, pop music was changing, as rock became something more adult, something more interesting and even, according to the tastemakers, something worthy. And the Stones themselves were also less confident, less strutting; possibly even fearful of what might be happening to them.

Brian's position was becoming increasingly untenable. He had long ago stopped being the leader (self-styled) of the band, having given up that role to Mick, initially, and later to Mick and Keith. Describing Brian's personal life as a mess implies it had the potential to be cleaned up. With numerous illegitimate children and a string of relationships with women who only ever seemed to understand parts of him and a hedonistic lifestyle, for which he appeared to have lost the use of the brake while simultaneously pressing down even harder on the accelerator, it meant that some kind of crash was inevitable.

"Five long-haired lads who will never figure in the list of Best-Dressed Men, look like romping up the pop ladder."– Daily Mirror, November 1963

We will never know all that happened between Mick and Keith and the rest of the band over Brian's situation as a Rolling Stone. It's quite likely they can't remember themselves all that went on during the later part of 1968 and early 1969. The truth always depends on who tells it, and in this case there were numerous different truths. But there's no question that the rest of the Stones wanted the band to go on, if only to make the kind of money that the world thought they already had. However, with Brian a liability, physically, emotionally and professionally, there was no just way he could stay.

For the last 40 years there have been stories and whispers from people saying that Brian wanted to leave of his own accord. This was probably true. He had lost his band mates along the way and he knew he was never going to regain control of the group that he had formed. Better to go and do the things you had always wanted to do and lead your own band, playing the music you loved rather than be a bit-part player.

And so it was, with summer just beginning, events were set in motion that could trace their cause to much earlier happenings, which would have such a profound effect not just on the Rolling Stones but also on the whole of rock music. Much of what had gone before came to a head in the heat of the summer. Brian Jones left the band he had founded to be replaced by the 20-year-old wonder-kid blues guitarist Mick Taylor who brought so much to the band but was initially and ultimately overwhelmed by where he found himself. Within a few weeks Brian died in the swimming pool of his Sussex farmhouse; his dreams were unfulfilled and a whole mass of conspiracy theories were spawned.

The Stones played their Hyde Park concert which was not the best gig they ever performed – far from it – but

have to become, Keith and Anita Pallenberg (Brian's former girlfriend) had a baby son, and the Stones announced a huge tour of America that was designed to put them back firmly centre stage; such was the demand for them that extra dates were added.

Come December at the Stones' finale to their tour – a massive free concert just outside San Francisco – things almost went spectacularly and horribly wrong. In the wake of Woodstock anything was possible, but not if you have the Hells Angels as your security and a crowd of half a million. Might the band have been injured, or worse? Quite possibly. Having escaped the horror of the Altamont concert on an overcrowded helicopter they might have failed to make it back to the city.

Life turns upon events, and the Rolling Stones survived to become the Greatest Rock 'n' Roll Band in the World, not

"When I'm 33, I quit. That's the time when a man has to do something else. I don't want to be a rock 'n' roll singer all my life. I couldn't bear to end up as an Elvis Presley & sing in Las Vegas. It's really sick. Elvis probably digs it. Not me." – Mick *Daily Mirror*, 5 August 1972

this was the dawn of the 'Greatest Rock 'n' Roll Band in the World'. On the afternoon of 5 July 1969 at around 5.25pm those words were uttered for the very first time, by way of introducing the band. Today that single phrase and the 'Rolling Stones' are completely interchangeable.

With Brian's funeral taking place less than a week after the Hyde Park gig the beat boom generation lost its first icon, a reminder to even those too young to think about such things that life really is that fragile. Mick Jagger went to Australia to further his career as the film star that he might

just because Sam Cutler called them that in Hyde Park in the summer of '69 and throughout the US tour. They have done so because of all that happened over those fateful 30 odd days, 40 years ago.

The Rolling Stones have gone on to be watched in concert by more people than any other band. They have come to epitomise everything that is excessive, exciting, powerful, lavish and brilliant about rock music. They are dynastic, imperial and majestic... true Rock Royalty.

One thing's for sure. We will never see their like again.

A Rock 'n' Roll Band?

The Rolling Stones was the brainchild of a blues fan who moved from Cheltenham to London in early 1962. Almost immediately after the move he set about getting a band together. By the time Brian had completed the band's line-up in early 1963 The Beatles were taking Britain by storm; pretty soon it would be the world. Ploughing a very different musical path, but inevitably following in their wake, was Brian's band. Neither he, nor the rest of the band and certainly not the public, could have begun to imagine just how big they would become.

"I hope they don't think we're a rock 'n' roll outfit."
– Mick Jagger, 7 July 1962

On a May day in 1962 the 20-year-old blues fan from Cheltenham, recently moved to London with **Alexis Korner**'s encouragement, held the first rehearsal of the band he was putting together. Brian Jones had booked a room at the White Bear pub, just off Leicester Square in London's West End. Initially it was an odd assortment of jazz misfits and blues wannabes, along with some rock 'n' roll refugees.

Around the same time, Alexis Korner invited a 19-year-old student from Dartford named Mick Jagger to sing with his group at their regular Saturday night shows at the Ealing Club, as well as on Thursdays at the Marquee Jazz Club in London. Brian's rehearsals switched to the Bricklayer's Arms in Soho; soon Korner was suggesting people to try out with his young protégé's nascent band. A pianist named Ian Stewart, who would for ever be known as "'Stu", had been at Brian's rehearsals almost from the start. Guitarist Geoff Bradford, who had a band called Blues by Six, tried out, as did Brian Knight, who sang with Geoff's group.

In June Mick Jagger turned up at one of Brian's rehearsals, followed a few weeks later by his mates from Dartford, Keith Richards and bass-playing Dick Taylor; the three of them had played together as Little Boy Blue and the Blue Boys. There was an urgent need for a drummer so Brian put an advert in the *Melody Maker*. It was answered by a young lad from Penge named Tony Chapman who

"He'd done his homework, and was deadly serious about the whole thing. He wanted to play Muddy Waters, Blind Boy Fuller and Jimmy Reed stuff."
– Ian Stewart

played in The Cliftons, a local rock 'n' roll band whose leader was a 25-year-old ex-RAF National Serviceman called Bill Perks. Chapman's claim to the drum seat was enhanced by the fact that he could play the shuffle beat that graced many of Chuck Berry's records; soon Mick was playing them his *Jimmy Reed at Carnegie Hall* LP, suggesting this was the kind of music the band should be playing.

When Alexis Korner's group was offered a BBC broadcast on the night when they normally played the Marquee he needed someone to dep. for his band so they wouldn't lose their regular slot. As reported in *Disc* magazine on 7 July, who better to sit in than "Mick Jagger and the Rolling Stones, together with another group headed by Long John Baldry."

"It was a terrible name. It sounded like the name of an Irish Show Band, or something that ought to be playing at the Savoy."
– Ian Stewart

Brian had decided on their name, although to begin with there was confusion as to whether they were "Rolling" or "Rollin'".

Over the course of the summer, before Dick Taylor quit to pursue his studies, they played sporadic gigs at the Ealing Club, the Marquee, the Woodstock Hotel in North Cheam and the Flamingo Jazz Club in Soho. By December Bill Perks, who was by this time calling himself Bill Wyman, had joined at the behest of Tony Chapman who, unbeknownst to him, was about to be fired. By January 1963, after much persuasion, drummer Charlie Watts was coerced into joining. The original line-up was complete. Brian, Mick, Keith, Bill, Charlie and Stu were the Rolling Stones.

•Opposite – *The Stones pictured backstage in late 1963*

During the opening months of 1963 the Stones played wherever and whenever they could, which was mostly clubs in and around London. They were paid, but the money was pitiful. Bill, Stu and Charlie had jobs, so for much of the time they subsidised the other three who were all living together in a filthy flat in Chelsea's Edith Grove. Along the way they acquired a quasi-manager, the wonderfully named Giorgio Gomelsky, the son of a Russian doctor and his French wife. For a while his plans for the band, which centred on their regular appearances at the Crawdaddy Club in Richmond's Station Hotel, seemed to be progressing well.

Then, on the last Sunday in April, enter Andrew Loog Oldham. The 19-year-old hustler and soon-to-be Stones' manager went down to the Crawdaddy and in the days that followed persuaded the band to sign with him and his partner, Eric Easton, an old school show-biz type. Brian even negotiated himself extra pay in recognition of his position as leader; he also agreed with ALO that Stu should be dropped from the line-up because "six was too many in a band". For the next three decades Stu would remain the trusted conscience of the Stones. The band signed with Decca Records – who had missed out on signing The Beatles – and on Friday 7 June their first single, a cover of Chuck Berry's 'Come On', hit the record shops; by the middle of the summer it had almost cracked the Top 20.

Initially Oldham tried to put the band in matching waistcoats and dogtooth jackets in an effort to conform to what was considered right and proper for all popular music groups – especially by TV executives. The Stones rebelled, loosing their new clothes or not wearing their new uniforms when they should; soon they were back to their normal scruffy selves. Oldham quickly understood that conforming wasn't the answer – being different was. Instead of a band that looked the part, he created a band that everyone's Mother loved to hate.

"In the back room there were about 500 people, in a place designed for 100. The music transformed them, they stood jammed together – it was like a ritual." – Patrick Doncaster, the *Daily Mirror*

•Opposite – *Andrew Loog Oldham*

One of pop's great myths is the so-called "battle of the bands" between The Beatles and the Stones. The "conflict" was great PR for both of them but it was the Stones who benefited most. Both bands were entirely different in the way they were presented to the public, although at the time

> "When The Beatles were having hit records and bridging the generation gap, the Stones were saying, you either like us or f**k off."
> – Andrew Loog Oldham

people were hardly aware of how music was marketed.

As their rivalry had hardly just begun an incident took place that exemplified just exactly what it was that made one so different from the other. The day after the Stones finished on the Everly's tour they drove 228 miles in their van to play in Preston, Lancashire. At about the same time

as they went on stage at the Top Rank, The Beatles were performing in London's Prince of Wales Theatre for the Queen Mother and Princess Margaret at the Royal Command Performance. While Mick was belting out 'Roadrunner' or 'You Better

Move On', The Beatles were doing 'Til There Was You' from the musical *The Music Man* – it was all a far cry from Hamburg. The following day the Stones played a 45-minute set to a wildly enthusiastic crowd in The Beatles' spiritual home, Liverpool's Cavern Club; hundreds were locked out. Three days later Lennon and McCartney's composition, 'I Wanna Be Your Man', which they had "given" to the Stones, first entered the charts.

The bands met for the first time in April 1963 when The Beatles stopped in at the Crawdaddy on their way

> "It was a real rave. The audience shouted and screamed, and danced on tables. The beat the Stones laid down was so solid, it shook off the walls, and seemed to move right inside your head. A great sound."
> – George Harrison

back from a TV show in Twickenham. The Beatles' third single, 'From Me To You', their follow-up to their February chart topper 'Please, Please Me', had just come out. They walked in during the Stones' first set. Bill Wyman later recalled: "I was staggered to see the four Beatles standing watching us from just 6 feet away. They were dressed identically, in long black leather coats. I remember thinking 'shit, that's The Beatles'." From then on they became good friends although their very different touring schedule meant they met up but rarely.

• Opposite – *6 July 1964, 'A Hard Day's Night' premiered in Piccadilly Circus, attended by Princess Margaret. There were scuffles in the street between Beatles and Stones fans. The Beatles held a party at the Dorchester Hotel where Brian and Keith turned up, seen here chatting with Paul McCartney*

"The essential difference between ourselves and the British groups that are well known in the USA at the moment is that we haven't adapted our music from watered-down music like white American Rock 'n' Roll. We've adapted our music from the early blues forms." – Brian Jones

The first time the Stones appeared on our TV screens was in July 1963, as guests on ITV's *Thank Your Lucky Stars*. A few weeks later they had a slot on *Ready Steady Go*, and in January 1964 they made it onto *Top of the Pops* to plug 'I Wanna Be Your Man'. In between there had been a tour with former American teen idols the Everly Brothers, along with Bo Diddley and Little Richard.

With 'I Wanna Be Your Man' rattling the door of the Top 10 they were playing somewhere in Britain virtually every night. A tour with the Ronettes in January was followed by another with John Leyton during which the Stones' cover of 'Not Fade Away', a homage to Buddy Holly by way of Bo Diddley, made it all the way to No. 3 on the UK charts. In April, after several more months of nightly gigs, the Stones' first LP came out; by May it had topped the charts. Next stop: America.

Contrary to popular myth the Stones were not at the forefront of the British Invasion of America. Indeed, their first tour was just nine shows in eight cities – at one show in Minneapolis there were just 400 fans; in Omaha 650 turned up. Bands like the Dave Clark Five and Freddie and The Dreamers were, to begin with, more popular than the

"We won't last for ever. We're having a ball now, but what will be happening in one, five, 10, even 20 years time. We'll start worrying when there are fewer fans than knockers." – Mick Jagger

Stones. But one Stone was proving especially popular with American men as well as women. Brian Jones, every inch the pop star, would be the inspiration for many wannabe beat bands in America. Just take a look at early pictures of the Byrds – who had their first hit 10 months after the Stones' tour – each of them with a Brian Jones haircut.

Home from America and 'It's All Over Now' topped the UK charts; gigs up and down the country were all close to turning into small-scale riots. By the time of their second US tour, which began in October, the US audiences were much bigger, thanks in part to the band cracking the US Top 10 with 'Time is on My Side'.

•Opposite – *Mick, Bill, Brian and Charlie and David Jones, the Chief Barker of the Variety Club of Great Britain at a luncheon at the Savoy Hotel on Thursday 10 September 1964 when the Stones were presented with the No. 1 Group Award*

•Previous Page – *The Stones on stage at Longleat House in Wiltshire on Sunday 2 August 1964*

At the end of 1964, having completed a second US tour, the Stones topped the UK singles chart with Howlin' Wolf's 'Little Red Rooster' – an out and out blues song proving they were no rock 'n' roll band. More success on the LP charts in both the UK and America was followed by a tour "down under", and in March 1965 'The Last Time' became the band's third British No. 1 in a row. Within two months they had completed another UK tour as well as jaunt through Europe, which they followed up with their third American tour. Then came the record that proved the Stones were a rock band: in the US '(I Can't Get No) Satisfaction' went to No. 1 and stayed there for a month; in the UK it managed to do the same but only for two weeks.

For the rest of 1965 it seemed as if the band were riding a whirlwind. It was gigs, promo, record releases, interviews and all the other attendant hoop-la that goes along with being one of the two biggest bands in the world. It culminated at the end of the year with a 37-venue US tour in 38 days in 20 different states – knackering even by today's standards, but in a world less sophisticated it sapped the band's energies. They had also transferred their bad boy image, so carefully cultivated by Andrew Loog Oldham, from Britain to America.

1966 brought little or no change to the band, other than they got more successful, but it did bring a change in their personal circumstances; Mick bought an Aston Martin,

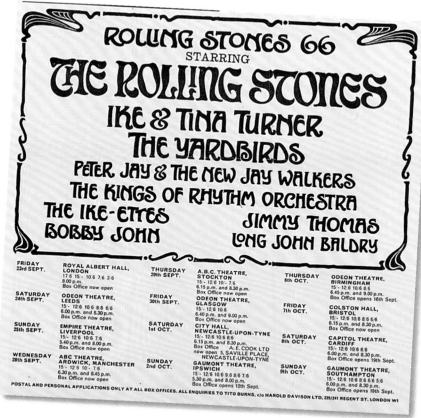

Keith a Bentley and Brian a Rolls-Royce. There were more hit singles, longer and bigger tours that took in Australia, New Zealand and Europe, a fifth US tour and a UK tour in which they were supported by Ike and Tina Turner and the Yardbirds. This year also marked the start of Mick's relationship with Marianne Faithfull, a love affair that would play itself out across the remainder of the decade.

"*With their jacknife profiles, junior Rasputin coiffures and cockney calls for 'girlie action', the Stones have been cast as the bad boys of popland. What people see is five hipless moppets dressed like carnival coxcombs, spread across the stage in rock-'n'-roll formation.*" – Newsweek, 29 November 1965

• Opposite – *Just before the first of two shows at the ABC Theatre in Belfast on 6 January 1965*

• Next Page – *The Stones at the London Palladium on 22 January 1967*

"Why should we have to compromise with our image? You don't simply give up all you have ever believed in because you've reached a certain age. Our generation is growing up with us and they believe in the same things we do – when our fans get older I hope they won't require a show like the Palladium." – Brian Jones, February 1967

After the disappointment of 'Have You Seen Your Mother Baby, Standing in the Shadows' which only got to No. 5 in the UK (No. 9 in the US), the Stones kicked off 1967, the spring of the "summer of love", with their call to 'Let's Spend The Night Together'. With Jimi Hendrix arriving on British soil, music was taking a very definite turn from pop to rock, which makes the Stones' decision to play TV's *Sunday Night at the London Palladium* a strange one. They refused to go on the revolving stage at the show's end and wave to the audience like show-biz muppets, but why did they bother going on in the first place? Their "scandalous" behaviour outraged the press and some of the aged among the glitterati.

Two weeks after the Palladium event the band found itself embroiled in a real scandal. After a February Saturday evening spent recording at Olympic Studios, Mick and Keith, along with Marianne, George Harrison, Patti Boyd and other friends headed to Redlands, Keith's Sussex farmhouse. At about 5am on Sunday the Harrisons left Redlands. Twelve hours or so later the police arrived and, as events unfolded, the Redland bust became the very stuff of which rock mythology is made. Mick and Keith were in serious trouble: by mid-March the press was full of stories of court appearances; and by May it was reality. Mick and Keith were to attend a hearing in Chichester.

Keith was accused of permitting his home to be used for the purpose of smoking cannabis resin. Mick faced a summons of being in unauthorised possession of four tablets of amphetamine sulphate and methyl amphetamine hydrochloride. Robert Fraser, another of the Redlands' guests, was accused of being in unauthorised possession of heroin. They all elected to go to trial in June. Meanwhile, in London, Brian was being busted at his flat in South Kensington; the police found 11 suspicious objects, including two metal canisters, two pipes, two cigarette ends and a chair caster obviously used as an ashtray. When detectives showed Brian one of the items, along with a phial bearing traces of cocaine, he was adamant it wasn't his.

On 27 June Mick and Keith were in court. Keith was sentenced first, jailed for 12 months and ordered to pay £500 towards costs. Mick was jailed for three months and ordered to pay £100. Both were taken to Brixton Prison before being released on bail the following day after a hearing. This was the beginning of a long slow end for Brian's band.

Feelings between Keith and Brian were bad because Brian's girlfriend, Anita Pallenberg, decided she preferred Keith. There was no degree of certainty that Mick and Keith would get off on appeal. Musically Mick and Keith seemed strangely short of new material and the band's relationship with their former Svengali, Oldham, was at breaking point.

Roll on the summer of love...

"Yes, it is hash. We do smoke. But not the cocaine man. That's not my scene. No man, no man. I'm not a junkie. That's not mine at all." – Brian

•Opposite – *Mick and Keith leaving Redlands on 27 June 1967 for their court appearance*

Daily Mirror

4d.   Thursday, September 14, 1967   No. 19,820

Drugs-trial quiz today, then final decision

2 'STONES' BARRED BY U.S.

Jagger, Richard in airport drama

From BRIAN HITCHEN, New York, Wednesday

ROLLING STONES Mick Jagger and Keith Richard were both refused entry to America tonight when they arrived at Kennedy Airport on different planes.

First to arrive was Richard. Immigration officers took the pop guitarist to a private room and questioned him for more than half an hour before they announced their decision.

They agreed to allow him a "deferred entry" examination at the immigration offices on Broadway tomorrow morning.

The same treatment was handed out to Jagger when he arrived later than from Paris.

The deferred entry examination means that the two stars must tomorrow answer questions about their drugs trial in Britain earlier this year.

Although they were denied official entry tonight, they were allowed to go to a New York hotel.

Information

Richard arrived at Kennedy Airport in a Trans-World jetliner with other Rolling Stones Bill Wyman Brian Jones and Charlie Watts.

The Stones were due to see their New York-based manager Alan Klein.

An immigration spokesman said that a decision on the two Stones would be made tomorrow "in the light of information requested from London."

Richard was sentenced to one year's imprisonment earlier this year for allowing his Sussex farmhouse home to be used for smoking Indian hemp.

The conviction was later quashed and the sentence set aside in the High Court.

Jagger was sentenced to three months for possessing four drug tablets but, on appeal, he was given a conditional discharge.

Manager Klein said tonight "The Rolling Stones went to discuss business and work on a new idea for a record album—that's all."

Rolling Stone Keith Richard at London's Heathrow Airport yesterday before he flew to New York.

TV team 'boards Caroline today'

By JAMES WILSON and KEVIN HUNT

A GRANADA television unit will board the pop pirate ship Radio Caroline today — despite all attempts to stop them.

A company spokesman said: "It is a secret plan and I cannot reveal how it will be done.

"But it will be done by a means which we believe to be legal."

It is thought that they may use a Dutch tug to put a team on board.

After filming material for "A World In Action" programme about Radio Caroline founder Ronan O'Rahilly, the team would be put ashore in Holland. Then they would be flown back to England.

Failed

The new plan was announced just after the trawler Ross Dainty berthed at Felixstowe, Suffolk, at 8.40 last night having failed to put a camera team on board the pirate ship.

Radio Caroline is one of two pirate ships still defying the Government's anti-pirate radio law. The other is her sister ship. Radio Caroline North, off the Isle of Man.

The Ross Dainty's bid was called off—after a 26-hour wait at sea — when Granada lawyers decided that the team might be committing a technical offence if they went aboard.

Even so, the company were prepared to have a go "in the interests of news gathering."

But the trawler's operators, Islandia Shipping Services Limited, were not willing to take the same risk.

AHOY!   Five men of the TV film unit aboard the trawler Ross Dainty wave as a Daily Mirror chartered plane flies overhead. Alisdair Macdonald took the picture.

"The Rolling Stones are one of Britain's major cultural assets, who should be honoured by the kingdom instead of gaoled."
– Allen Ginsberg, letter to *The Times*, 12 July 1967

Support for Mick and Keith came from many people, some of it surprising, including William Rees Mogg's famous piece in *The Times*. As editor he wrote a defence under the headline 'Who Breaks the Butterfly on the Wheel'. The music business, at least the bands and artists, were united in their support of the pair. Mick and Keith's appeal was put back to the end of July, while the BBC demonstrated their total grasp of the concept of the summer of love by threatening to edit Mick and Keith out of The Beatles' 'All You Need is Love' promo film to be shown on *Top of the Pops*; Brian Epstein was incensed. "I would object most strongly if cuts were made from the film. The Beatles want Mick and Keith in."

With all this going on around Mick and Keith the music for once took a back seat. They were often absent from the studio when Brian, Charlie and Bill were there to work on tracks for a new album. Brian was also absent for a while, having checked himself into the Priory Clinic to get help for his drug problems.

On 26 July Robert Fraser's conviction was upheld – not a good omen for Mick and Keith. Then, on July 31, with Mick in court and Keith in a side room because he had chicken pox, Keith's conviction was quashed. Mick's was upheld but his sentence was quashed. They were free. But there were worrying issues to confront. With a drug conviction would Mick be allowed into the USA? For the band there was another issue: Brian was rumoured to be leaving. During interviews some members questioned whether the Stones had a future. The insecurity surrounding the band was not helped by the fact that difficulties between Andrew Loog Oldham and

their new Svengali, Allen Klein, were coming to a head.

In mid-September the band flew to New York to shoot the cover for their new album, *Their Satanic Majesties Request*. At JFK airport US Immigration officials initially refused Keith entry, then relented and allowed him "deferred entry". Mick, having been in Paris with Marianne, flew on a later flight, but met the same fate. The following day they were given permission to stay for three days, though were told that US Immigration would decide whether they would be allowed in again after they studied the reports of their cases.

A month later Brian appeared in court, where he pleaded guilty to possessing a quantity of cannabis without authority and permitting his premises to be used for the smoking of cannabis. He was jailed for nine months on the latter charge, with a further three months for possession of cannabis. Following his appeal, in mid-December he was up before Lord Chief Justice Parker and two other Law Lords, who heard a medical testimony confirming that a prison sentence would affect him so deeply that he was potentially suicidal. Instead, Brian was given three years' probation.

A long drawn-out end was reaching a crucial phase...

"We split because we all got to a stage of mutual boredom."
– Andrew Loog Oldham

The Cheltenham Blues Boy

Born into a middle-class family from Cheltenham, that bastion of middle England, Lewis Brian Hopkin Jones should have been the epitome of respectability. Instead he got the blues, went off the rails early on and struggled to stay on them for the rest of his 27 years. Yet he was a natural musician whose only musical failing was his inability to write the kind of music he liked to play.

"He could have easily joined another group, but he wanted to form his own. The Rollin' Stones was Brian's baby."
– Keith

He was born at the Park Nursing Home in Cheltenham, Gloucestershire, on Saturday 28 February 1942. His parents, Lewis and Louisa, lived in Eldorado Road in Cheltenham, Lewis senior was an aeronautical engineer with the Dowty Group, and Louisa taught piano; Brian's parents were Welsh, having met and married in Bridgend in 1938 before moving to Cheltenham in 1939. They both loved music; Brian's father played the piano and the organ as well as leading the choir at their local church. Their interest in music was passed on to their son; but little could they have imagined how events would turn out.

his 11-plus and in the following September he began at Cheltenham Grammar School; Brian was the third grammar-school Stone, along with Mick and Bill. Shortly after his 14th birthday, "Buster" Jones as he was known, became first clarinet in the school orchestra. The following year he got seven O-levels and in 1957, with England in the grip of the skiffle craze, Brian entered the sixth form. He was there to study physics, chemistry and biology, following in the footsteps of his father, who had a B.Sc. in engineering from Leeds University.

Of course, had Brian taken other subjects his life might have turned out differently and there never would have

"Musically I was guided by my parents. Later, there were several piano teachers in Cheltenham. I struggled to get the notes right early on, but eventually I found I had a 'feel' for music. I guess I knew that I was going to be interested only in music very early on." – Brian

When Brian was three his sister Pauline was born; sadly, she died two years later from leukaemia. In 1946 another girl was born, Barbara. In 1948 Brian started to learn the piano from his mother and would continue until he was 14.

Brian's parents were affluent enough to send him to one of Cheltenham's fee-paying junior schools where he excelled in music and English. In July 1953 he passed

been the Rolling Stones; it's on such detail that history hangs. Brian really enjoyed his two years in the sixth form. He found his niche and while in the lower sixth he got two more O-levels before passing A-levels in physics and chemistry. Given later events it will come as a surprise that he failed his biology A-level. Then again it might not, because despite an IQ of 135 he sometimes demonstrated a complete lack of understanding when it came to certain aspects of life.

"I encouraged him to take science subjects at A-level when his heart wasn't really in it. Perhaps if he'd taken other subjects, he would have followed a more orthodox career." – Lewis Jones

•Opposite – *Brian on 6 July 1964*

CHELTENHAM SPA
A BEAUTIFUL RESORT
IN THE HEART OF THE COTSWOLDS
Illustrated Guide free from Dept. D.R. Town Hall Cheltenham

When Brian was 15 or 16 he heard his first Charlie Parker record and as a result persuaded his parents to buy him a saxophone. This proved, like many things with Brian, to be a passing phase, and for his 17th birthday he was given an acoustic guitar. It was shortly after this that Brian's first child was born. He had had a fling with a 14-year-old schoolgirl from Cheltenham: though Brian wanted her to have an abortion, she chose to have the baby, which was then adopted. And after leaving school, and much against his parents' wishes, Brian got a job instead of going to university.

Brian left Cheltenham and in August 1959 moved to London, where he got a job working for a company that made spectacles. However, it was only a matter of weeks before he quit and went back to Cheltenham, where he picked up odd jobs, spending more and more time playing with various local bands. In September he hitchhiked to Scandinavia with friends, taking his guitar so that he could busk.

On his return he went to a see a band play at the Wooden Bridge Hotel in Guildford, Surrey, where he met a young married woman; after a one-night-stand she became pregnant. This produced the second of Brian's children, although he had no further contact with her as she and her husband stayed together to have the baby. Just before Christmas 1959 Brian was in a Cheltenham coffee bar where he met 15-year-old Pat Andrews. The two started going out and Brian got a job in a local factory. He then started work in a record shop, Curry's in Cheltenham High Street, which went bust soon after he joined.

All this time Brian had been living at home, but at some point late in 1960 he and a mate moved into a large bedsitting room in Cheltenham, along with two art students. A month or so later Pat Andrews found out she was pregnant; again Brian wanted his teenage girlfriend to

"I quite honestly didn't feel much of an urge to do anything else except play music. I thought about different jobs and rejected them, I knew I'd be bored stiff."
– Brian

have an abortion, but Pat wanted the baby. For Brian there was no question of marriage; his independence meant too much to him. On the work front, a job as a junior architect for Gloucester Council lasted no time at all; Brian then applied to Cheltenham Art College, was accepted but when someone wrote anonymously to say he was "irresponsible and a drifter" the college quickly withdrew their offer.

Brian's third child, a baby boy, was born to Pat Andrews on 23 October 1961. They called him Julian Mark, after Brian's latest favourite musician, Julian Cannonball Adderley. The couple did not live together and for the most part Brian acted as if he was free and single. One night he went to see the Chris Barber Band in Cheltenham Town Hall; their set included a blues segment featuring Alexis Korner. Afterwards the two of them talked. It was another of those moments that helped make history.

"I met Brian in Cheltenham. Brian came into the dressing room to talk. Not about the band set, but the blues set."
– Alexis Korner

•Opposite – *Brian Jones with Anita Pallenberg, December 1965*

In the weeks running up to Christmas 1961 Brian went to London and stayed with Alexis Korner, who played him an Elmore James record. Brian was so excited by what he heard that he bought a single pick-up Harmony Stratotone electric guitar as soon as he got home; a converted tape recorder acted as an amplifier.

"I discovered Elmore James, and the earth seemed to shudder on its axis." – Brian

Brian became obsessed by the blues, practising slide guitar while listening to Elmore James and Robert Johnson records. In January 1962 he met another 19-year-old, Paul Pond who lived in Oxford and had his own blues group. Paul would later change his surname to become Paul Jones, the original lead singer with Manfred Mann. Brian almost joined Paul's blues band but the arrangement fell through when it became clear that Brian wouldn't be leader. This didn't stop the two blues fans from recording a tape together, though, as Elmo and Paul, when Brian crashed at Paul's place on his way to and from London.

Brian would often hitchhike to London, sometimes with a mate, to go to clubs. He was in London the night that Alexis Korner and Blues Incorporated played their first show at the Ealing Club. Besides Alexis on electric guitar and Cyril Davies on vocals and harmonica, the band included drummer Charlie Watts. Brian gave Alexis the tape that he and Paul Pond had made; he also asked for the chance to play at Ealing.

On Korner's second week Brian turned up with his guitar and sat in with Blues Incorporated; Charlie was there too. By late March the club was getting a name for itself and on 31 March *Disc* magazine said "By word of mouth the news had spread and people flocked to it from all parts of London – some came from as far afield as Sevenoaks and Cheltenham." On 7 April 1962 Mick, Keith, Dick Taylor and a friend, whose father lent them his car, went to Ealing where they saw Brian sitting in with Alexis playing slide guitar on Elmore James' 'Dust My Broom'.

"He was the first person I ever heard playing slide electric guitar. Mick and I both thought he was incredible." – Keith

After the show Mick and Brian talked for the first time; Brian mentioned he was forming a band...

ALEXIS KORNER'S

BLUES INCORPORATED

THE MOST EXCITING EVENT OF THIS YEAR

RHYTHM AND BLUES CLUBS No. I

EALING CLUB. Ealing Broadway Station, turn left cross at Zebra, go down steps between A.B.C. Teashop and Jewellers.

This Saturday and every Saturday at 7.30 p.m.

No. 2 MARQUEE CLUB, 165 Oxford Street, London, W.1. Grand Opening This Thursday (May 3rd)

•Opposite – *Brian backstage at the London Palladium on 22 January 1967*

"We wouldn't bother to get out of bed some days, as there was no heating in the flat. I didn't see the point in getting out of bed just to get cold. We put all our clothes into a communal kitty."
– Brian

When Brian first moved into Edith Grove with Mick and Keith they all got on really well. Everyone's focus was on securing as many gigs as possible – Brian and Keith didn't have a job and Mick was at the London School of Economics, so money was tight. Even getting to gigs was difficult; they had to go on the bus, which meant that most of the places they played were in and around London. Brian was also seeing a new girl, Linda Lawrence, although she would be shuffled off the scene when Pat Andrews and Julian came to visit; eventually Pat and the baby moved into a flat in Ladbroke Grove.

On 11 March the Stones did some demos at IBC Recording; their three-hour session on a two-track machine produced versions of Bo Diddley's 'Road Runner', 'Diddley Daddy', Muddy Waters' 'I Want To Be Loved', Jimmy Reed's 'Honey What's Wrong' and 'Bright Lights, Big City'. This was what Brian wanted the Stones to be – a blues band. Brian was more proud of these recordings than anything else he did with the band.

It was Brian who first met Giorgio Gomelsky, and when Andrew Loog Oldham came along it was Brian who took the lead in negotiations – he was, after all, the leader. While Keith and Mick waited around the corner in a Lyons Corner House, Bill, Charlie and Stu were all at work; Brian signed a contract with Oldham and his partner Eric Easton. Brian then reported back to the others, including the bombshell that Stu was to be dropped from the line-up to become their "road manager". What Brian didn't tell them all was that Eric Easton thought Mick's voice was weak and that it wouldn't last on the road: "I'm thinking of replacing him," said Brian.

A few days later the Stones played a gig in Battersea Park – their first gig in a London park. As Pat and the baby were there, Brian walked around with Julian in his arms. Andrew was incandescent, telling Brian it would ruin the band's image if people knew he had a child. Shortly after this Brian, on behalf of the band, signed a recording contract with Oldham and Easton's Impact Sound Company; Impact released the Stones' recordings to Decca and received a 14% royalty of which the five Stones got 6%, Oldham and Easton 8%.

By the summer Pat Andrews went back to Cheltenham with Julian, leaving Brian to Linda Lawrence. A few weeks later Brian collapsed from nervous exhaustion and missed a gig at Windsor's Ricky Tick Club – it was not the last time that he would let them down.

STUDIO '51
10/11 GT. NEWPORT STREET
LEICESTER SQUARE (Tube)
Rhythm and Blues
every FRIDAY, 8.0
JOHNNY MAYALL BLUES BREAKERS
SUNDAY AFTERNOON
4 till 6.30
and every
MONDAY at 8
THE ROLLING STONES

"Brian was a lot more conscious of his background and what his family thought of him than the rest of us."
– Keith

•Opposite – *Brian sitting at the Mellotron in Olympic Studio in Barnes on 17 May 1967 where the Stones were working on 'We Love You' and 'She's a Rainbow' from Their Satanic Majesties Request*

In September 1963 Brian moved in with Linda Lawrence and her parents in Windsor, which marked the beginning of Brian's demise as leader of his own band. He wasn't around and the growing bond between Mick and Keith grew stronger in his absence. With Oldham's insistence that the band write their own songs, Mick and Keith knuckled down – whereas Brian seemed incapable of writing anything other than 'Moon in June' ditties. To add to the rift, Brian took Linda along to some gigs, which angered the others, especially Mick, since they felt this could dent their image.

Another blow to Brian's standing with the others came when they found out he'd been getting an extra £5 a week as leader of the group. According to Keith, "When we discovered this everybody freaked out, and that was the beginning of the decline of Brian." He needed the money, though: in December he found out that Linda was pregnant. Unsurprisingly, when Brian's parents found out they were very unhappy. Linda wrote: "When Brian wrote and told them about it, they denied it and cut me right off. They thought I was terrible because I was pregnant, but they'd accepted me before. I had slept in their house. It wasn't the way they expected it. I felt very bad, and Brian freaked out." There was a lot of freaking out in the sixties.

While Brian was staying with Linda's parents he had difficulties in containing his jealousy and on one occasion after a party he gave her a black eye. Not that his attachment stopped him from doing his own thing: soon after this incident, another girl whom Brian was seeing discovered she was pregnant. Then, in late April 1964, the inevitable happened; Brian moved out of Linda's parent's home and got a flat of his own. He met yet another girl,

"Keith and Mick were quite prepared to go along with anything Andrew said. They fed off each other." – Stu

Linda Keith, with whom he started a relationship, although he was still seeing Linda. At the end of July Linda Lawrence had a baby boy – and he, like Brian's other son, was also named Julian Mark. This was followed by another son in October, to the girl Brian had been seeing while still with Linda; it was his fifth illegitimate child. This time the mother had the baby adopted.

By December 1964 Linda Lawrence and Brian split up for good; this was the final straw for Brian and the start of his very personal slippery slope. Some have said that she was the love of Brian's life, but he just could not control himself. His relationship with Linda Keith continued until he met Anita Pallenberg on 14 September 1965 in Munich during the interval between shows; her German parents brought her up in Rome before she became a photographer's assistant in New York and later a model. Two months later Brian invited Anita to join him in Miami where the Stones were in the middle of their fourth US tour.

It was the start of the relationship that quite probably destroyed Brian.

"Brian really wanted to contact them. He would play his music for them. His mother didn't really listen, but Lewis tried to." – Linda Lawrence

• Opposite – *Brian at Heathrow Airport in August 1967 with photographer Michael Cooper*

• Previous Page – *Brian, The Beatles, Donovan (next to Brian) and Cilla Black standing behind Grapefruit, a band signed to The Beatles' Apple label, 18 January 1968*

Changing Times

Published at the end of every year, the *New Musical Express (NME)* of December 1967 was far from good reading for the Stones. Whereas they had been running The Beatles a close second they were now a distant fourth place in the world vocal group section, behind The Beach Boys and The Monkees and only just ahead of the Bee Gees. Times had well and truly changed; for the band and for Brian his three-year probation for possession of drugs was very bad news.

"Their Satanic Majesties Request, despite moments of unquestionable brilliance, puts the status of the Stones in jeopardy." – John Landau, critic, February 1968

While *Their Satanic Majesties Request* was about as successful as the band's previous album, *Between the Buttons* – they both reached No. 3 on the UK album charts – the Stones' singles output was well below par. 'Let's Spend The Night Together' made No. 2, but 'We Love You' only just got into the UK Top 10. Things in America were somewhat worse. They hadn't managed a Top 20 record on the billboard chart since 'Ruby Tuesday' at the start of 1967; *Their Satanic Majesties Request* made No. 2, but it was a success based on past glories, not hope for the future.

Everyone associated with the Stones had just one thing on their mind: would US Immigration allow Brian, Mick or Keith into America? Not that Brian seemed to be worrying too much; for him life seemed to be going along as normal. He had the windows of his Rolls-Royce blacked out and an eight-track stereo tape player fitted. The strain of the previous 12 months was certainly taking its toll, though: at one point he collapsed in his Chelsea flat and was found by his chauffeur. He was taken to hospital but refused to stay more than an hour. Brian did what was probably the most sensible thing in the circumstances, he left the country and went on holiday to Ceylon (now Sri Lanka) with his new girlfriend, Suki Potier. She was the former girlfriend of Tara Browne, the Guinness heir, who was killed in a car crash in London in December 1966 and was immortalised by The Beatles in 'A Day in the Life'.

Back from Ceylon Brian went along to Olympic Studios where Jimi Hendrix and Mitch Mitchell were working on Bob Dylan's 'All Along the Watchtower'. Also there was Dave Mason, who played acoustic guitar with Hendrix while Brian played percussion. For some reason Noel Redding had left the studio so Hendrix played a Framus bass that had once belonged to Bill Wyman; he had given it to Andy Johns, the assistant engineer on the session.

Meanwhile Brian was faced with a bill of almost £9,000 for legal costs following his court case; the average annual wage in Britain at the time was around £1,000. Contrary to what many people thought, and despite the obvious trappings of success like the Rolls-Royce, Brian's finances meant that his lavish spending constantly drained the Jones' bank account (along with Bill and Charlie, he did not accrue the song writing royalties that Mick and Keith did).

A few days before Brian's 26th birthday the Stones

"Oh yes. We are hoping to make several live appearances shortly from our wheelchairs. In fact, I think you can safely say that live appearances are a thing of the future." – Mick, 26 February 1968

began running through some new songs at a rehearsal studio in south London that Mick and Keith had been writing; they needed to get back into the recording studio to stem the tide of under-performing records.

"I was feeling terribly exhausted and fainted. I'm much better now, and that is why I didn't stay in hospital." – Brian, *Daily Mirror*, 15 December 1968

• Opposite – *Backstage in May 1968 prior to their appearance at the NME Poll Winners Concert; they won best R&B group*

"We'll be in the studios during March and April. We hope the sessions will also produce a new single. I think the Stones are a fantastic group, but I must admit I have preferred some of their early stuff to the last album." – Jimmy Miller, *Disc*, 2 March 1968

In an effort to freshen up their recording mix the Stones had decided to work with a new producer. Their choice was Jimmy Miller, a 26-year-old American, who had come to Britain at the invitation of Chris Blackwell of Island Records to work on Spencer Davis' 'Gimme Some Loving', as well as with Nirvana, Spooky Tooth and Traffic. One day at the rehearsal studio Bill was playing an electric keyboard while he was waiting with Brian and Charlie for Mick and Keith to turn up. Charlie and Brian were playing along to the riff he had found; according to Bill it was "really good and tough". When Mick and Keith arrived they both agreed: "it sounds great, and don't forget it." It was the riff to 'Jumpin' Jack Flash'.

Keith had made a demo of a song on his new cassette recorder. The homemade recording sounded really good so it was put onto the four track to which the band added overdubs. Originally called 'Primo Grande', the song became 'Street Fighting Man'. Recording tracks for the new album, some of which failed to make the final cut, continued throughout March and April; sometimes Brian was there but as often as not he wasn't. However, the band was all together when Michael Lindsay-Hogg made a promo film for 'Jumpin' Jack Flash' at Olympic Studios.

Bill's riff, which morphed into 'Jumpin' Jack Flash', was just what the Stones needed to silence the critics. In fact it just did the opposite, since when it came out the critics went from criticizing to praising the band in the blink of an eye. It is arguably the most important single of their career; they

needed to put themselves back on track with the fans. Anything less than a big selling record would have been a severe blow.

On 12 May the Stones went to the Empire Pool in Wembley to play the NME Poll Winners Show on a bill that included Status Quo, The Association, Scott Walker, Amen Corner, The Herd, The Move, Dusty Springfield, and Cliff Richard. It was a surprise appearance at which they played both their new single and 'Satisfaction'; Dave Dee, Dozy, Beaky, Mick & Tich closed the show.

"An important release for the Stones which will prove one way or the other whether they are still a major chart force. My guess is they've got a number one with the most commercial Stones single in a long, long time." – Melody Maker

•Opposite – *On stage at the NME Poll Winners Concert at the Empire Pool on 12 May 1968. The last time Brian ever appeared in concert with the band*

"The boys now feel the time is ripe for more personal appearances. But any future Stones' concerts will be of an entirely different nature from the traditional pop show format."
– Stones' spokesperson, *NME*, 18 May 1968

The Wembley appearance was all part of a marketing offensive designed to put the Stones firmly back in the public eye for what they were really all about – the music – rather than their personal problems, most of which were drug related. As 'Jumpin' Jack Flash' came out the Stones' publicist issued an invitation. "The Rolling Stones invite you to meet them at 46a Maddox St, London W1 on 15 May at 3.30pm. We have arranged this magazine and periodical conference with the Rolling Stones to afford you the opportunity of interviewing them." This was more like a royal summons than an invitation from a pop group. After the press conference the band and their birds all managed a collective night out to see *2001 – A Space Odyssey*; probably their first in many years.

Just as things appeared to be going along smoothly, Brian was once again at the centre of a mini maelstrom. Not long after 7am on the morning of 21 May he was woken up by policemen knocking at the door of his Chelsea home; ominously, they had a warrant. Brian didn't open the door immediately and when they eventually gained entrance through a hatchway they found Brian sitting on the floor dialling his solicitor. "You know the scene, man. Why do I always get bugged?" was all that Brian could offer.

After finding various things at the flat that could be related to drug-taking Brian was taken to Chelsea police station where he was charged with possessing a quantity of cannabis. The arrest was part of a carefully concerted police campaign, as evidenced by the search warrant. Brian was completely frazzled by what had happened, and after being granted bail later that day he went to stay with Keith at his house in Sussex; Mick was there too, and they better than almost anyone understood Brian's predicament.

All this somewhat overshadowed the release of 'Jumpin' Jack Flash', which came out on 24 May. However, it soon recovered and went to No. 1; the band's first in the UK for two years. Released in America a week later it climbed to No. 3; their biggest hit in over 18 months.

"I am not the leader of the Stones. Charlie is the leader of the Stones, and I wouldn't attempt to usurp his authority in any way. When he makes a decision, we stick by it."
– Mick, *Disc*, 8 June 1968

•Opposite – *Brian leaves court with girlfriend Suki Potier after he was found guilty of possessing cannabis on 26 September 1968*

"I will state till my death that I did not commit this offence."
– Brian, 26 September 1968

Beggars Banquet, the Stones' new album, was so named by the Stones' old friend Christopher Gibbs, who came up with the idea while decorating Mick's new Chelsea home; the name inspired an idea for a cover. The band rented a house in Hampstead in which they staged the banquet, which was photographed and became the inner sleeve of the album. A couple of weeks later the Stones agreed to appear in Jean-Luc Goddard's film *One Plus One*: they were featured working on 'The Devil Is My Name', which was later renamed 'Sympathy for the Devil'. Their contract with Goddard included a clause about the possibility of Brian failing to appear in the film as a result of his drug case; the point highlighted the growing practical difficulties of the band's situation. By early June Brian was back to court, where he elected to go for trial by jury in September.

During the summer the band holidayed in various parts of the world; Brian was in Tangier and Marrakesh while Mick and Keith were in Joshua Tree National Park in the California Desert with Gram Parsons, of the Flying Burrito Brothers, along with Marianne and photographer Michael Cooper hanging out and having their photographs taken. Back from holiday Brian went to court where, much against the odds, he was released with just a small fine. This was a huge relief; he must surely have expected to be sent to prison given the fact that he was on probation for his earlier offence.

This latest court case could have been the end of the Stones, as the public knew them, but in fact the band actually got down to making music. There were rehearsals aimed at getting the band fit to go back on the road. With their new album in mind they tried, unsuccessfully, to hire the Tower of London for the launch. Instead they settled on the Elizabethan Rooms at the Gore Hotel, at 190 Queensgate in Kensington.

The Stones' own "Beggars Banquet" for 70 invited guests from the media took place at lunchtime: the event was as over the top as the inside cover of their album, with serving

Rolling Stones

Beggars Banquet

R.S.V.P   *Price 10/6*

"Not quite the sort of party I'm accustomed to, but thoroughly enjoyable." – Lord Harlech

wenches and food and drink in abundance. Near the end of the lunch Mick stood up: "Well, I hope you've all had enough to eat and drink. And I hope you've all enjoyed yourselves. But we didn't invite you here just to eat and drink and enjoy yourselves, did we?" At which point he picked up a meringue pie and slapped it in Brian's face, who was sitting beside him. An all-out food fight ensued, led by the Stones but including the principal guest, Lord Harlech, Chairman of the British Film Board.

A week before the Beggars Banquet the Stones appeared on television performing 'Sympathy for the Devil' on *Frost on Saturday*; it was to be the last time that they appeared on TV in their original line-up.

•Opposite – *The Stones before the fun started on 5 December 1968*

"A tour, with us on stage for 20 minutes or half an hour, kicking off with 'Satisfaction.' That's all finished. We are developing some ideas we've had for some shows that are different. They may be just crazy ideas, but they involve a circus." – Keith

The idea for the Rolling Stones' *Rock and Roll Circus* had been in the ether since early summer. Mick had turned their somewhat crazy notions into a concept for a TV programme. By the middle of November the *Daily Mirror* were first to break the news "The Stones are to produce their own TV spectacular – for sale all over the world. They will star in an hour-long show, which will cost £20,000 to make. Worldwide sales are likely to earn them about £250,000."

With the budget rapidly escalating to £32,000 ($700,000 today) it at least promised to be spectacular. Michael Lindsay-Hogg, who had filmed the 'Jumpin' Jack Flash' promo film, was brought in as director with plans well advanced, including clowns, animals and dwarfs all hired from Sir Robert Fossett's Circus.

On 9 December, a few days after the release of *Beggars Banquet*, rehearsals for the *Rock and Roll Circus* began at a London hotel; joining the Stones were Taj Mahal and his band, Stevie Winwood, Eric Clapton and Marianne Faithfull. At lunchtime the following day a press call at the film studios included the Stones, The Who, John Lennon along with Yoko and his son Julian, and Eric Clapton.

After the press call, rehearsals and filming began; Yoko was dressed as a witch, The Who, Jethro Tull, clowns, a tiger in a cage were all there along with Mick who was dressed appropriately as a ringmaster; the rest of the Stones looked as if they had raided a theatrical store. Besides all the rock 'n' roll artists was the classical pianist Julius Katchen, who played Brahms and the Israeli violinist Ivry Gitlis, who performed Paganini's 'First Violin Concerto'.

John Lennon, Eric Clapton, Mitch Mitchell (drummer with Jimi Hendrix experience) and Keith Richards played 'Yer Blues'; they were christened the Dirty Mac band. Later John, Mick and Eric played 'Peggy Sue' while Lennon did a wry version of Elvis' 'It's Now or Never'. The Who ran through 'A Quick One, While He's Away' and then Ivry Gitlis played Paganini's concerto. After about five minutes the director shouted "Cut!" Gitlis was furious: "How can you cut a violin concerto in the middle of a movement like that?"

The following day they were back, and, after numerous stops and starts, at around 1am the <u>next</u> morning the Stones finally began filming their segment. Everyone had been there for hours and the energy gradually slipped away after take after take on each of their songs. They did at least three of 'Jack Flash' and six of 'Sympathy for the Devil'. The filming was finally wrapped up around four in the morning.

When Mick saw the 'rushes' he cancelled the showing to the TV companies and insisted the Stones' segment be re-shot. While budgets were drawn up for the reshoot nothing ever happened and the great rock 'n' roll experiment lay in the vaults for over 25 years.

"We decided to put up the money for the spectacular ourselves so that we had complete control of the production. We have never tried producing a show before. If we aren't pleased with the result we will scrap it." – Mick Jagger

• Opposite – *Bill, Charlie, Keith Moon of The Who and Brian stand behind Yoko, Julian and John Lennon and Eric Clapton of Cream during rehearsals for Rock and Roll Circus*

• Previous Page – *After the fun started*

"Right now I feel I'm old enough to get out of the group scene and go into something completely different." – Mick in *Teenbeat* Annual, released at Christmas 1968

1969 began with *Beggars Banquet* reaching No. 3 on the UK album charts, the same position as their previous three albums. In the USA it could only manage No. 5, not even as good as *Their Satanic Majesties Request*. The band themselves were taking a break. Brian went again to Ceylon with Suki Potier, visiting Arthur C. Clarke, the author of *2001 – A Space Odyssey*. Back home there was extensive press speculation about the band's proposed US tour scheduled from late March to early May. Naturally it was the uncertainty around Brian's position that concerned the Stones' management office – would he be allowed in? The Stones' lawyers were consulted, and also about the need to inform the American Embassy that they were applying for a visa for Brian. The overriding problem was that Brian's appeal against his latest drugs conviction was thrown out in late January. This all but ruled him out of a US tour.

For the Stones the issue revolved around their ability to continue as a cohesive group. Without an American tour record sales would drop dramatically, a fact underlined by the relatively poor performance of *Beggars Banquet*. Money was becoming an issue for the band as a whole, not helped when Allen Klein took over the running of The Beatles Apple Company.

By February they were back at Olympic studios to start recording once again, their tour plans on hold. In various interviews the band were beginning to talk about putting their US tour back to the end of the year to give themselves time to sort out the increasingly complex logistics of large-scale tours, as well as Brian's visa. There was also the possibility of a show at the Coliseum in Rome.

No sooner had the band begun working on songs, like 'Let it Bleed' and 'Midnight Rambler', as well as adding a choir to 'You Can't Always Get What You Want', than trouble with Brian was back at the top of the agenda. The pictures of Brian from the *Rock and Roll Circus* showed him looking far from well, and despite his holiday in the Far East he was back in the Priory Clinic in Richmond; his health was again an issue. Added to this his relationship with Suki was breaking down, which put a strain on his psyche.

Brian's behaviour after he came out of the Priory became even more erratic. One day he borrowed the group's Jaguar and went shopping in Pimlico Road; the car was towed away, so he simply hired a chauffeur car to take him home to his new house in Sussex. A month or so later he crashed his motorcycle into the window of a shop near his house; he was admitted to hospital under an assumed name to avoid publicity.

Not that Brian was the only one in trouble. At the end of May Mick and Marianne were arrested and taken to Chelsea Police Station after drugs were found in their Cheyne Walk home following a police raid. Later that evening the Stones finished working on 'You Can't Always Get What You Want'.

Life reflecting art?

•Opposite – *Brian with model Donyale Luna, who played the part of the fire-eater's assistant in the Rock and Roll Circus. This was his last public appearance as a Rolling Stone*

The End or the Beginning?

It had reached crisis point. Somehow things would have to change or the band could no longer go on. Brian was increasingly detached from the other Stones and, most importantly, the music. Both could perhaps be solved, but if Brian was not to be allowed back into America there was no way the Stones could tour. And if a US tour was out of the question the band would probably come to an end. In contrast to today's scene, bands in those days had to tour in order to sell records – and it was record sales that filled the coffers.

"I no longer see eye to eye with the others over the discs we are cutting. We no longer communicate musically. The Stones' music is not to my taste anymore." – Brian

Just days after the announcement that Mick was going to appear in a film about Ned Kelly's life he was arrested, along with Marianne, charged with possession of drugs. It seemed as if there was a concerted police campaign against the Rolling Stones; after all, they were not the only band in London smoking cannabis, but the Stones were the only ones to be regularly arrested. The issues with Brian took a temporary back seat when Mick and Marianne went to Marlborough Street Court to face charges; they were remanded on £50 bail and another potential nail banged into the coffin of a US tour.

When Brian was no longer musically integral to the Stones, no one was unhappier with this than Brian. It had got to the point where for the Stones to survive Brian would have to leave the band he had formed, but long ago lost control of to Mick and Keith. It was Stu who came up with a replacement for Brian; he recommended a young guitarist named Mick Taylor.

Mick Taylor came from Welwyn Garden City in Hertfordshire, and at 20 years old he was a good deal younger than the rest of the Stones. He had taught himself to play guitar when he was 12; three years later he left school and started work as a commercial artist-engraver. His first band was a local group called The Gods that included Ken Hensley, who later played with Uriah Heep. Mick T. got a call from John Mayall in May 1967 asking if he'd like to join his Bluesbreakers as a replacement for Peter Green – Mick was 17. During his two years with Mayall the band toured extensively, and when Mayall moved to Hollywood Mick also lived in Los Angeles. He was featured on three classic Mayall albums, *Crusade*, *Bare Wires* and *Blues From Laurel Canyon*. In March 1969 Mick left Mayall to do his own thing – his timing was perfect.

Mick Jagger phoned Mick T. and told him that Brian was thinking of leaving and asked him along to a Stones' session at Olympic on Saturday 31 May. They worked on 'Live With Me', and obviously Mick. T fitted in well as Keith said, "see you tomorrow" as they were leaving. The next evening they worked on 'Honky Tonk Women'; the Stones had been trying to nail this song for some time. At around 11pm the five of them got down to business. The session initially didn't go well, until Jimmy Miller moved Charlie off

> *"I definitely added something to Honky Tonk Women, but it was more or less complete by the time I arrived. I played the country kind of influence on the rock licks between the verses."* – Mick Taylor

the drum seat and showed him a rhythm that he thought might work. It did, and by 3am next morning they had got a great take and an hour later a rough mix. It was Charlie's 28th birthday, and the Stones had their new single and a new guitarist.

"Mick Jagger will star in a big-budget film to be made on location in Australia. Mick will play a swashbuckling rose as the 19th-century folk hero bandit Ned Kelly." NME, 24 May 1969

• Opposite – *Mick and Marianne leaving Marlborough Street Magistrate's Court on 29 May 1969*

• Next Page – *The Stones with new guitarist Mick Taylor, in white, photographed in Hyde Park on 13 June 1969*

"We will continue to be friends. Obviously you cannot break up a friendship after so long." – Mick

There was just one problem. The Stones had not talked to Brian. Over the next few days work continued on finishing 'Honky Tonk Women'. Then, on the evening of Friday 6 June Keith and Anita Pallenberg were driving home from Olympic Studios when Keith crashed his Mercedes near Chichester, eight miles from Redlands. Keith escaped unhurt, but Anita broke her collarbone. The car was a write-off. Keith was undoubtedly lucky to have escaped unhurt.

Over the weekend rumours began to spread about Brian leaving the Stones; this was not the first time and so no one got very excited by the news. When Brian was contacted he dismissed the rumours. "There is no row. Everything is all right between us. It seems as though someone is spreading a rumour."

On Sunday 8 June Mick, Charlie and Keith spent the afternoon at Olympic working on some mixing; Bill was not there; he had stayed home at his Elizabethan manor house in Suffolk. After being called at home by the press

"I have a desire to play my own brand of music rather than that of others, no matter how much I appreciate their musical concepts. We had a friendly meeting and agreed that an amicable termination, temporary or permanent, was the only answer. The only solution was to go our separate ways, but we shall still remain friends. I love those fellows." – Brian

and having denied there was any split, Brian phoned the studio. Almost on the spur of the moment, perhaps because they knew something had to be done, and that previously no one could quite face up to the reality of their situation, the three Stones drove to Sussex to see Brian. They arrived in a little over an hour and had a 30-minute talk with him; it was apparently amicable and no one got upset.

The facts were simple. Brian was not going to get a work permit allowing him to perform in America; the Stones had to be able to tour. There was also the question of Brian's health; he had increasingly been to see doctors and his visits to the Priory Clinic were becoming more frequent. Perhaps most telling of all, and particularly as demonstrated on 'Honky Tonk Women', the Stones were no longer a blues band: they were not and had not been for a long time the band that Brian had created.

In the end Mick, Keith and Charlie agreed that Brian should make a statement and that everyone would stick to the story. Later that evening it was officially announced that Brian had left the Stones, and it was confirmed that Mick Taylor was taking his place in the group.

"The Rolling Stones' photo call to introduce the 'new' Rolling Stone. Mick, Keith, Bill and Charlie invite you to meet their new lead guitarist Mick Taylor at a photo call. The Date: Friday June 13th. The Place: The Bandstand, Hyde Park (on the edge of the Serpentine nearest Hyde Park Corner). The Time: 2.30pm."

The Stones did a photo shoot with American photographer Ethan Russell on Thursday 12 June in which they dressed in American uniforms; there were also a number of models dressed as hookers – their honky tonk women. Later that day Mick had a meeting with Blackhill Enterprises about the Stones doing a free concert in Hyde Park.

Around lunchtime the next day all the Stones convened at their office before being driven to Hyde Park for the photo call to introduce Mick. T, arranged by Leslie Perrin, their PR man. The following day's papers were full of reports of the press call. Calling Mick Taylor a guitarist with "Byronic looks", many concentrated on the fact that he'd gone from £100 a week to £1,000 practically overnight.

The following Wednesday the Stones went to the Mayfair Theatre to record a segment for David Frost's American TV show. The band mimed to backing tracks of 'Honky Tonk Women' and 'You Can't Always Get What You Want', while Mick sang live. The show aired at the beginning of July; it was the first time America saw a Brian Jones-less Stones.

For Mick and Marianne there was the small matter of having to go back to court on the drugs charge. They did so on 23 June, at which a new hearing date was set for late September. The judge had taken a lenient view because of the filming of *Ned Kelly*, although in Mick's eyes it seemed that Australia might not welcome him with open arms: an Australian MP was being urged by his constituents to have him banned from appearing in a film about their national treasure. The MP had contacted the Minister for Immigration, requesting that Mick should be refused entry. According to one of the protestors, "Jagger is nothing like the bronzed Anzac image Australians have of Ned Kelly. To think of this hairy ass playing Ned Kelly... ugh!"

Meanwhile, on Friday 27 June plans for the Hyde Park free concert were released to the press. There was no sense in giving people too much notice.

"Rolling Stones' Free Concert in Hyde Park on July 5th. After consultation with the Ministry of Public Building & Works, Blackhill Enterprises have received permission to stage a free concert in Hyde Park on Saturday July 5th, which will star the Stones. Announcing the concert this week the Stones' office said 'No final arrangements for the rest of the bill have been made but those who attend the concert will have a total of 5hrs non-stop entertainment completely free of charge'. The concert will start at 1pm & will be held in the 'Cockpit' area of the Royal Park."

• Next Page – *The Stones in Hyde Park on 13 June 1969*

• Page 72/73 – *Mick Taylor strolls away from the press conference in Hyde Park on 13 June 1969*

The Soul of the Stones

Brian Jones' somewhat nomadic existence, in which he lived in a series of London flats and mews houses, came to an end in November 1968 when he bought Cotchford Farm, near Hartfield, East Sussex. It was here that A. A. Milne and his family took their holidays, and the surrounding area is the setting for both *Winnie-the-Pooh* and *The House at Pooh Corner*. There's even a statue of Christopher Robin in the garden. Milne's fictional character never grows up, and in many ways nor did Brian. This was where Brian's life tragically ended; for some his death still seems shrouded in mystery.

"You'll never make 30, man." – Keith

"I know." – Brian

At the beginning of August 1968 Brian and Suki Potier were staying in Marrakesh. Brian wanted to make a recording of Moroccan musicians, including the Master Musicians of Jajouka in the Atlas Mountains. Brian, Suki Potier and George Chkiantz, a recording engineer whom Brian had flown out to help him, were standing on the hotel balcony in Marrakesh when Brian suddenly slumped to the floor. While George was shocked Suki assured him that it was nothing out of the ordinary and all they needed to do was to get Brian to bed, which they did, and he would be back to normal after he had slept. Home from Morocco Brian, who had been looking to move out of London for a while, drove to Sussex with Suki to look at a farmhouse that was on the market for £31,500 (around £800,000 today).

Cotchford Farm was about 50 miles from London. Parts of the house are thought to date back to the 13th century. The farmhouse had two reception rooms, a breakfast room, six bedrooms, a garage block and a staff flat; outside were ornamental gardens, a paddock, and 11 acres of woodland. It also had a swimming pool. Brian fell in love with the house as soon as he saw it and decided to buy it.

In September negotiations stalled somewhat during Brian's court appearances, but by November, after some haggling over the price, Brian finally bought the farmhouse for £29,500; during the first week of December he began moving in. At about this time Marianne Faithfull went into a nursing home; a few days later she had a miscarriage. She had been seven months pregnant with a baby girl whom

"Brian could easily get out of the business altogether... he is ambitious enough, but really lacks the ruthlessness needed to be a 'lifer' in show-business."
– *Teenbeat* Annual, 1969

she and Mick had planned to name Carina.

Brian first began living at Cotchford at the time of the *Rock and Roll Circus*. He usually hired a chauffeur-driven car for his trips to and from London, since he had sold his Rolls-Royce a few months earlier. He bought antiques from Christopher Gibbs, and began renovating the farmhouse. There were also some issues over the swimming pool that Brian had his builder, 44-year-old Frank Thorogood, look into; it had not long been built so was still under guarantee. A crack was found on the bottom of the pool, and so the company who installed it agreed to repair it free of charge.

"Brian is in Morocco taping local folk music for release on stereo LPs later in the year. He is staying at Morocco's most expensive hotel the 'El Minzah', and returns in September to face trial at the Inner London Sessions." – *Disc*, 17 August 1968

•Opposite – *Cotchford Farm*

"He (Brian) had been drinking. He was a bit unsteady on his feet. They were in no condition to swim. I felt strongly about this and mentioned it to both of the men." – Janet Lawson

After the announcement that Brian was leaving the Stones all attention was on the band's immediate future – the Hyde Park concert, Mick's filming in Australia and speculation about their America tour. One night towards the end of June Brian turned up at Olympic, where the band were recording. According to Bill, "there was no doubt that Brian was excited about his musical freedom". It was a future that Brian thought could include joining his old mentor, Alexis Korner and his band. Korner visited Brian and Anna Wohlin, who had by now replaced Suki Potier as Brian's girlfriend, at Cotchford. They talked about Brian joining Alexis' band, but Korner encouraged him to do his own thing; perhaps he sensed that Brian was not ready, or perhaps it was all about Brian being the leader again.

By the beginning of the summer of 1969 the swimming pool at Cotchford had been fixed, which was just as well because the weather in early July was hot and humid. It was particularly so on the evening of Wednesday 2 July; the temperature had hovered at 80 degrees all day. It was the worst kind of weather for asthma, from which Brian had suffered all his life. Since moving into the farmhouse Brian spent the early part of the evening in the music room, which he had installed. At around 8.30pm he and Anna were joined by Frank Thorogood and his 22-year-old girlfriend, a nurse named Janet Lawson (the two of them were staying in the staff flat). Brian's friend Tom Keylock, one of the

Stones' roadies, had recommended Thorogood to do the renovations at Cotchford.

After eating dinner the four of them sat down to watch *Rowan & Martin's Laugh-in* with their guest, the singer Abbe Lane, on BBC2. After this came *The Bobby Gentry Show* with Alan Price. When it was over at around 10.30pm Brian decided to have a swim and suggested they all did. Janet thought they had been drinking too much and warned them against it, but the other three went ahead. Brian put on a multi-coloured pair of swimming trunks while Anna wore a black bikini. Frank joined them in the heated and lit, blue-tiled, pool while Janet sat and watched.

Brian was obviously the worse for wear and even had trouble getting onto the springboard, so Thorogood had to help him. After about 20 minutes Anna and Janet went back into the house leaving the two men in the pool; Frank followed them about 10 minutes later, for a cigarette. Janet, worried about Brian, went back outside where she saw him lying, motionless, at the bottom of the pool. "I sensed the worst and shouted to Anna and Frank."

Thorogood dragged Brian to the edge of the pool where Anna helped pull him out of the water. They laid him on his side and Janet immediately began to pump a little water out of him; she then massaged his heart for 15 minutes. The following day Anna told friends that she was sure Brian was still alive when they got him out the water. After Janet

Daily Mirror

5d.   Thursday, July 3, 1969   No. 20,378

3.30 am LATEST   *Drama of pop guitarist*

BRIAN JONES OF THE 'STONES' FOUND DEAD

Strike chaos today on the Tubes

By ALAN LAW

MOST of London's Tube trains will be at a standstill today because of an unofficial one-day strike by 253 men.

The snap stoppage was called last night by Underground signalmen involved in a pay dispute. They acted against union advice. And they plan to strike every Thursday until the dispute is solved.

More than 2,000,000 people travel by Tube every day. Road chaos is expected, because many of them will switch to cars to get to work.

A London Transport spokesman said: "It is impossible to say how many trains we can run, but every line is likely to be affected.

"There are certain sections where the signalling is completely automatic and we hope to have trains running on these sections.

"What the overall effect of the strike will be it is impossible to say."

Offer

The decision for the wildcat strike was made by ninety men meeting in a canteen at King's Cross Station.

It was unanimous. And it will have the support of all the 253 signalmen on the Underground.

After the meeting, Mr. Bob Kettle, a member of the National Union of Railwaymen's national executive committee, read a statement on behalf of the men.

It said: "We reject the further offer of the London Transport Board and will strike tomorrow and each subsequent Thursday until satisfaction is achieved."

Mr. Kettle said that he went to the meeting to urge members to accept London Transport's offer.

The offer was an extra 27s. a week as part of a pay and productivity deal. One proviso was that the number of signalmen should be reduced by two—to 251.

Mr. Kettle said the two men would be given jobs in another section.

The new offer was 4s. higher than one made last week. But the signalmen want 30s.

FOR ANN.. TENSION AND TRIUMPH

Ann Jones yesterday . . . in her finest victory.   Picture by MONTE FRESCO

THE pressure is on . . . and the strain and tension of the big occasion shows in the face of Ann Jones.

But so, too, does the grit and fierce determination that have long made her Britain's most consistent tennis player.

This was how Ann looked on the Centre Court at Wimbledon yesterday as she conquered the No. 1 seed, Margaret Court, to reach the final for the second time in three years.

It was the finest victory of Ann's long and distinguished career and she owed it, she said later, to a secret thought halfway through her 122-minute semi-final with Mrs. Court, the Australian.

Ann had lost a marathon first set. Then, she said: "I had a private thought and I'm not about to tell you what it was. But it seemed to work."

In fact, it worked superbly. For Ann, who is thirty, scorched her way through the last two sets to win 10—12, 6—3, 6—2.

For Margaret Court, twice a Wimbledon cham-

pion, it was the end of the road.

She said: "I shan't come back again. I intend to settle down and become a full-time housewife."

What The Mirror Says,
Page 2; Peter Wilson—
Page 22

BRIAN JONES FOUND DEAD

BY DON SHORT

POP guitarist Brian Jones, who quit the Rolling Stones last month, was found dead early today.

His body was discovered by friends who called at his £30,000 home at Hartfield, Sussex.

It is believed to have been in the swimming pool, at the house which 25-year-old Jones moved into a few months ago.

The Rolling Stones tour manager, Tom Keylock, phoned me early today and said: "I got a call from Brian's house, and the voice said there was trouble at the house. But when I rang Brian back there was no reply, and I am extremely worried."

When I broke the news, Keylock said: "This is a terrible shock. I spoke to Brian yesterday morning and he was full of spirits and raring to go."

Pressures

Jones had been the most controversial member of the Rolling Stones since they were formed in 1962.

He was twice convicted on drugs charges and during his court appearances it was stated that he had been under psychiatric treatment for "pressures and tension."

His parting from the Rolling

Body found by his friends

Stones came in a sudden announcement last month.

He said: "The Stones' music is not to my taste any more. I want to play my own kind of music.

"We had a friendly meeting and agreed that an amicable termination was the only answer."

Group leader Mick Jagger said: "Brian wants to play music which is more his own rather than always playing ours.

"We have decided he is best to be free to follow his own inclinations. But we part on the best of terms."

Friendship

"We will continue to be friends. Obviously you cannot break up a friendship after so long."

Jones said he would devote his future to a new musical unit he was about to form.

Since he moved into the new house he had given one or two small parties for close friends. But mainly he kept to himself, working on his own musical project.

Keylock said: "I can't say what his plans were. But he was full of enthusiasm about them."

The Rolling Stones have just cut their first single record without Brian Jones. The disc called "Honky-Tonk Women" is being released tomorrow.

had tried to get his heart going Anna tried the kiss of life, after which Frank gave him artificial respiration, but there was no reaction. While all this was going on one of them dialled 999 and later still Thorogood called Tom Keylock. Tom's wife phoned Olympic where the Stones were working, to tell Mick what had happened.

As soon as the ambulance men arrived they tried to revive Brian; after about 30 minutes they gave up. Anna later told Bill Wyman that the ambulance men did not appear to take the incident seriously and they were very slow in doing anything to help him. Meanwhile, Detective Inspector Ron Marshall, head of East Grinstead CID, arrived at Cotchford. A little later a local doctor pronounced Brian dead.

• Next Page – *Cotchford Farm on the morning of 3 July 1969*

• Page 81 – *Janet Lawson followed by Anna Wohlin at Cotchford Farm on the morning of 3 July 1969*

"It just does not seem fair that he's dead before he really got a chance to grow up. Well, at least now he does not have to work so hard at living." – Pat Andrews, 13 July 1969

About two hours after Brian had been dragged from the pool Leslie Perrin was woken with the news. The Stones' PR man immediately dressed and drove to Cotchford. While the police were taking statements from Frank Thorogood, Anna and Janet, the ambulance men took Brian's body to East Grinstead, where at about 3am Detective Inspector Marshall made a statement to the Press at the police station. It was shortly after this that Leslie Perrin and Tom Keylock arrived at the house. The Press were already gathering. Perrin later made a statement on behalf of the band and Brian's family: "Brian's father, and all members of the Stones had been informed, and all had expressed shock." Anna, who was also in shock, finally got to bed about 5am, while in the early morning light Keylock and Perrin inspected the pool area. According to Perrin, "We found Brian's 'puffer' (Inhaler) on the side of the pool. We gave it to the police."

The following day Anna Wohlin joined Bill Wyman and his Swedish girlfriends in London while Janet Lawson went home to her parents in Lincolnshire. Arrangements were made for Brian's three spaniels and his Afghan to be taken to local boarding kennels. Brian's body remained at Queen Victoria Hospital in Holtye Road, East Grinstead, where Dr Albert Sachs performed an autopsy. He reported drowning, drugs and liver degeneration. Dr Angus Sommerville, the local coroner, was informed of Brian's death and the date of the inquest was set for Monday 7 July, just two days after the Hyde Park concert.

At the inquest it was reported that Brian had had pleurisy. His heart was larger than it should have been for a 27-year-old, while his liver was twice the normal weight. There was no evidence of an asthmatic attack but there were signs of chronic bronchial trouble. Having questioned all the witnesses the coroner stated: "He would not listen. So he drowned, under the influence of alcohol and drugs." The verdict was "misadventure".

Ever since Brian's death there have been countless rumours, stories, conspiracy theories and books a-plenty offering every theory imaginable as to the circumstances of his death; there's even been a film. In 1993 Frank Thorogood was reported to have made a deathbed confession to Tom Keylock, saying he killed Brian. Keylock later told the police that he did not confess. In 2008 Janet Lawson told Scott Jones that her evidence to the police was not entirely true, however, she died of cancer before it could be investigated further.

We will never ever know the truth of what happened between the time Thorogood was left with Brian in the pool and Janet Lawson found him motionless in the water.

• Above – *Tom Keylock*

• Opposite – *The press talking to Tom Keylock outside Cotchford Farm on the morning of 3 July 1969*

"If Keith and Mick were the mind and body of the Stones, Brian was clearly the soul." – Rolling Stone, 9 August 1969

"It's a very weird life. We can't understand that kind of adulation. The Beatles and Stones were subjected to it with the greatest intensity but they survived it. You become some kind of spokesman for your generation. You're expected to be some kind of philosopher and you're not." – John Peel, 3 July 1969

"As a musician he should be remembered for the brilliant bottle-neck country guitar work on 'Beggars Banquet', for his interpretation of blues – played honestly as a white man." – Jimmy Miller, 12 July 1969

"He always seemed to be losing out one way or another. A little bit of love might have sorted him out. I don't think his death is necessarily a bad thing for Brian. I think he'll do better next time. I believe in reincarnation." – Pete Townshend of The Who, 3 July 1969

"He was one of those people who are so beautiful in one way, and such an asshole in another." – Keith, July 1969

"Brian was weak, had hang-ups and at times he was a pain in the arse. But he named us, we were his idea and he chose what we played when we were starting out. We were Brian's band and without him our little blues band wouldn't have become the greatest rock 'n' roll band in the world." – Bill

"He was the hardest boy in the world to understand and I think we all believed we could understand him if we tried long enough... But no one ever could."
– Pat Andrews, 3 July 1969; Brian's former girlfriend talking of Brian's insecurity and the need to have girls around him all the time.

The Stones in the Park

It was not the first, certainly not the last, nor was it probably the best, but it's the Hyde Park concert that everyone talks about. Ask anyone of a certain age if they were at the Hyde Park concert and they will instantly know which one you're referring to. There were many things that made it both unique and special, and although Brian's death a few days earlier changed little of what happened on stage, it did cast a very special shadow over what turned into a very British affair.

"The Stones want to play tonight for Brian." – Sam Cutler, Blackhill Enterprises introducing the band

Open-air concerts on a large scale were not particularly new but the sheer size of the Stones' Hyde Park concert marked it out from others. It was also free, which again was not unique, but no one expected quite so many people to turn up, and at such short notice. How much Brian's death made a difference to the numbers of people it's impossible to know; perhaps his passing helped to make it the very-laid back affair that people remember with such fondness, even if some of them struggle to recall much of the detail.

It was the jazz festivals at Newport Rhode Island in the USA during the 1950s that were the inspiration for the sixties' outdoor festivals. Jazz impresario George Wein established the Newport Jazz Festival in July 1954 at an old open-air casino: around 6,000 people turned up for the opening night. In Britain there had been small-scale open-air events that might just have passed for festivals, and these too were organised by jazz enthusiasts. But by 1963 these were changing, and the Richmond Jazz & Blues Festival featured the Rolling Stones at its opening night before the more staid tones of Chris Barber and Acker Bilk took over. As the years went by the size of festivals grew larger – determined by technology; it was no good just seeing a band, you had to be able to hear them as well, so the PA system had to be powerful enough to do the job.

1969 was THE year of the festival – the benchmark from which all others have been judged. Across North America and Britain there seemed to be a festival happening somewhere almost every weekend of the summer. The first of the festivals in '69 was in Canada, the Aldergrove Beach Rock Festival that bizarrely starred the New Vaudeville Band and Guitar Shorty. In Britain the first Hyde Park show starred Eric Clapton's new band, Blind Faith; Richie Havens was the first on stage in front of 120,000 people.

"The idea of having free pop concerts in Hyde Park came to Peter Jenner, a director of Blackhill Enterprises – the organisation which is promoting the concerts – after he saw open air pop shows in California."
–Newspaper report, 4 July 1969

On the same weekend as the Rolling Stones played Hyde Park the Atlanta Pop Festival attracted 140,000 who were regaled by the likes of Creedence Clearwater revival, Led Zeppelin, Blood Sweat & Tears and Ten Wheel Drive, among a packed two-day bill.

Just a month after the Stones in the Park, another festival, Woodstock: the Aquarian Music and Art Fair that was billed as three days of peace and music, took place and for ever cast its mythological shadow across both rock and festivals. People in America talk of the "Woodstock Generation" – in Britain we should talk of the "Hyde Park Generation".

•Opposite – *A small selection of the crowd in Hyde Park, with the Serpentine in the background*

"I came off stage shaking like a leaf because I felt that, once again, I'd let people down."
– Eric Clapton

On Saturday June 7, the day after Keith and Anita's car crash on their way home to Redlands, Mick and Marianne went to Hyde Park. Blind Faith headlined a free concert organised by Blackhill Enterprises. Blackhill was run by Peter Jenner and Andrew King, who were stalwarts of the London underground scene, having helped start the UFO club in Tottenham Court Road. Jenner had been a lecturer at the LSE, where Mick had been a student, and Blackhill ran their five-person business out of a converted shop just off Ladbroke Grove. They were principally agents, and it was their acts that gained most from the Hyde Park concerts, which gave them a higher profile than they would have expected from flogging around Britain laying low-key gigs. When Blackhill first approached the Ministry of Public Building and Works in 1968 about the possibility of staging concerts in the park they were met with a resounding "no". However, their persistence paid off, and on 29 June 1968 Pink Floyd headlined, supported by Tyrannosaurus Rex, Jethro Tull and Roy Harper.

The Blind Faith concert was the first of four concerts scheduled for 1969. Opening the show was the Third Ear Band along with Richie Havens, Donovan and the Edgar Broughton Band (no festival seemed to be complete without them).

It all kicked off about 2.30 and despite a crowd of 120,000 turning up on a really hot day it was barely reported by the national press and not much noticed by the pop press either. With the exception of Richie Havens, who as usual thrashed the living daylights out of his guitar, the bands never seemed to ignite the crowd. Perhaps they were anticipating guitar pyrotechnics from Eric Clapton, who along with Ginger Baker, Stevie Winwood and Rick Grech had formed Blind Faith, the new "supergroup", a tag with which they had been saddled to describe the musicians' pedigree. They kicked off with 'Well All Right' before going on to perform most of their debut album. As a nod to Mick, who stood watching from the side stage, they also did 'Under My Thumb'.

Having watched the Blind Faith show, soaked in the vibe and seen how many people there were watching, Mick decided that a free concert in Hyde Park to promote their new single and get them back in the public eye would be just the thing for the Stones.

"True, they weren't as polished as Cream had been, but then again I don't think there's anything wrong in master-musicians playing a bit of a 'woolly' set. That's what good rock 'n' roll is all about. Play it a bit raw. Fluff up a bit here and there. Make mistakes. Who cares?"
– Richard Evans, designer who later worked at Hipgnosis

• Opposite – *Most of the gear Blind Faith and the others used belonged to Clapton and Baker's old band, Cream*
• Next Page – *The Blind Faith concert from across the Serpentine*
• Page 94/95 – *Blind Faith on stage, Rick Grech far left, Ginger Baker at the drums*

"I don't see a great change in our sound. I mean, can you remember the records Brain played lead on? No, not our earlier ones – the later ones." – Mick rehearsing at Apple for the Hyde Park gig

It was the day after the Blind Faith gig that Mick, Keith and Charlie drove down to Cotchford to end Brian's time with the Stones. Did Mick talk about seeing Blind Faith? It would be surprising if he didn't. More to the point, was it all nicely timed and meticulously planned by Mick and Keith? Mick told the *Melody Maker* a couple of days later about the Blind Faith concert. "I thought they were very nice. I was right at the back of the stage and couldn't see them, but I thought somehow they were very strained. I guess they'll get more together and Ginger was fantastic. He's a beautiful drummer – the best drummer I have ever heard."

The day before Mick T. was introduced to the press Mick met Blackhill Enterprises to talk about the Stones doing a show in Hyde Park. The biggest hurdle was getting the Royal Parks Commission to agree to the gig. Once Blackhill had secured the go-ahead for the show the next, and arguably, the biggest challenge was the Stones getting their own act together. For many years they had been the tightest band on the road, but it had been a long time since they had played together on stage and of course never with Taylor. Prior to the Hyde Park show their last live show concert was the NME Poll Winners Show a year earlier – they did just two numbers. Before that it had been a European tour in April 1967. In reality, Hyde Park was to be their first concert in over two years.

• Opposite – *Donovan, left, grooving to Blind Faith*

• Previous Page – *Blind Faith with Stevie Winwood far left, and Eric Clapton next to him*

Rehearsals began in the afternoon of 21 June at The Beatles' studio in the basement of their Apple offices in London's Savile Row, and continued on and off until the end of the month. They didn't often last very long and, as was reported by at least one journalist, Keith was frequently late. They were hoping to do a dozen songs, many of which the Stones had never before performed live. Mick and Marianne's court appearances interrupted rehearsals. Little that happened in the run-up to the concert was ideal preparation for what was to be one of the most important gigs of the Stones' career.

The Stones were still in the studio when they heard the news of Brian's death in the early hours of the morning of 3 July; all except Bill, who had already gone back to the

"The Rolling Stones' free concert in Hyde Park is now expected to become a memorial tribute to Brian. Despite his departure from the group, friendships with other members remained close." –
Daily Express, 4 July 1969

Londonderry House Hotel where some of the band were staying in the build-up to the concert. Around lunchtime that day the Stones met up at their office to go to the BBC's Lime Grove studio to record a segment for *Top of the Pops*. They performed their new single which, by all accounts, was all a bit flat – which is hardly surprising. Earlier in the day Mick went shopping; he was looking for something to wear to a party. He called fashion designer Michael Fish who told him he had just the thing – a Greek-inspired voile dress that he was happy for Mick to borrow. Mick went along to Fish's shop on Clifford Street, just off Piccadilly, to pick it up and that evening wore it to a "White Ball" at

the home of Prince Rupert Loewenstein, who would later become the band's manager.

Friday was the official release date of 'Honky Tonk Women' and 'You Can't Always Get What You Want', and so the timing of the concert was perfect. In an interview a couple of days earlier Mick told a newspaper why the band were doing a free concert. "There's no money at all to be made out of concert-tours in Britain so we may as well do it for nothing. People think there's a fortune in touring, but I never made any money out of it. The expenses are phenomenal. But by asking us why we're doing it you're looking at it from the wrong angle. We want to do it. It's fun to play. It only becomes work when we have to do it day in day out."

According to Mick, the concert was also to be a showcase for their new album; interestingly, *Let it Bleed* would be their next album, *Sticky Fingers* was the one after that. "There will be some new things, too, from our next album *Sticky Fingers*. We've hired a whole lot of African drummers for the end of 'Sympathy For The Devil' because we want the sound to get very primitive. That should be a gas."

"We will do the concert – for Brian. We have thought about it an awful lot and feel that Brian would have wanted it to go on. He was music. I understand how many people will feel – but now we are doing it because of him."
– Mick, 4 July 1969

The evening before the concert the Stones were back at Apple for one last rehearsal, although Mick was suffering with laryngitis and probably the effects of a late night at the 'White Ball' the previous evening.

As the Stones rehearsed small groups of fans began to gather in Hyde Park in order to get the best positions for the concert itself. Several hundred were encamped in the area known as the Cockpit, the – by now – traditional spot in the park where the stage was erected. It was a natural dip in the ground, which gave the maximum number of people a half decent view of the stage. At around 11pm someone called for two minutes of silence in Brian's honour; then, at midnight, rather than closing the park as was usual, the police took a lenient view, deciding to let it remain open. As one policeman told the *Daily Mirror*, "We're not going to move them out tonight. They're behaving themselves, so why should we?"

As the night wore on some fans got a little over-excited and deck chairs were broken. Fires were lit, around which people danced carrying flaming torches; the fire brigade were called to deal with one fire that got somewhat out of control. Several fans were arrested and a handful were charged with minor offences. By morning almost 7,000 fans had made their way into the park.

Those arriving very early and those waking up viewed the final preparations. From the very first free concert in the park, Blind Faith's included, the stage was only about 3 or 4 feet high at the very most. For the Stones a new stage had been built that was closer to 10 feet high, which gave the band some added protection, but most of all gave it enough height so that more people could see the band. Instead of a PA system being accommodated on the stage itself, two 20-foot towers were built on each side of the stage allowing a much larger PA system to be accommodated. However, what ever they did would not allow everyone to

"We have made adequate arrangements. Although we're expecting a large crowd, we don't think there will be any trouble. Everything went quite smoothly at the last concert." – The Police

get a good view. According to Blackhill's PR man, "I think everybody will be able to hear, but only about 75,000 will be able to see." And whereas previous free concerts had cost around £600 to stage, this one cost five times that amount (around £60,000 in today's money).

Mick wanted the stage to be carpeted so that he could dance barefoot; he also wanted palm trees placed on stage, which was no problem. However, his request for parakeets proved impossible to solve. Even then no major outdoor festival would be complete without a special VIP area, and so immediately in front of the stage a section was cordoned off with crash barriers to house the Stones' special friends, families and anyone else who knew someone well enough to blag their way in. In a unique, yet prescient move, 50 Hells Angels were drafted in by Blackhill to deal with security. They certainly made sure they got the best positions to watch the show and there's a certain irony about their presence, given what would happen almost five months to the day at the Stones' free concert at the Altamont Raceway in California.

• Next Page – *The backstage area from across the Serpentine*

• Page 106/107 – *The Hells Angels acting the part of Security*

"I was around 18 and from East London. I had that name on my jacket with a dragon. We weren't Hells Angels; we were the Forest Gate Greasers. We all liked the band, so about 10/12 of us turned up the night before and slept out in the park. We weren't Hells Angels, but there were some of them there. There was one tall thin guy called 'Wild Child'; he had a Nazi helmet and was doing a lot of shouting and strutting about, but there weren't too many of them there." – Stefan Gradofielski, a Greaser

As the morning wore on, and with the concert due to start at around 1pm, the crowds grew steadily and by 11am the police reckoned there were 25,000 people in the area immediately in front of and around the stage. Many more were just enjoying themselves in the hot sun in other areas of the 350-acre park. People stripped off for a dip in the Serpentine and before too long many of the ice cream sellers and soft drink vendors were seeing their stocks run low. The humidity made it uncomfortable, but the Hells Angels in their outrageous swastika-ridden clothes and their Second World War Nazi helmets seemed to be impervious to the heat; maybe it was all part of some weird ritualistic initiation.

The so-called Hells Angels seemed to spend most of their time strutting around the VIP enclosure in front of the stage demanding of the press, and others, their special blue access passes. However, according to Nick Logan in the *New Musical Express*, "The press enclosure would have had us believe that 80 per cent of our papers are represented by 16-year-olds with Brownie cameras." According to Mick Farren, the only person who seemed not to need a pass was Allen Klein, who "looked like a gangster from a Martin Scorsese film". At this point no one knew who Scorsese was, but a month later he was helping to film *Woodstock* and on his way to cult status.

The approaches to the park were filled with people flocking from every direction; most arrived by train from around the London area, or tube or bus if they lived in the city itself. There were also many fans who made the trip from all over Britain. Among the crowd were two former students from St Martin's School of Art who wandered around striking their now familiar poses. This was one of the first public appearances of the acclaimed artists Gilbert and George.

Since first light camera crews had been setting up their gear and capturing the scene in the park for a documentary that was being made by Jo Durden Smith for Granada TV. There was plenty for them to film, long before any of the bands took to the stage, since by lunchtime the crowd had swelled to around 200,000 people. It was by far the largest gathering of hippies, music fans, teenagers and the great and the good of British counter-culture, such as it was, that had ever gathered together in one place.

•Opposite – *Gilbert and George in their grey, worsted suits*

"There was a definite sense of occasion as we took the stage and hit 'Schizoid' for the thousands of British hippies and devotees of contemporary culture laid out on the grass before us in a seemingly endless ocean of colour." – Ian McDonald of King Crimson

Over at the Londonderry the Stones and their entourage were gathering. Bill and his girlfriend had a suite and it was there that the rest of the Stones began congregating from around lunchtime. The talk was all about Brian. Mick and Marianne left their home, along with Nicholas, Marianne's son, at around 2.30pm; Mick's laryngitis was still bothering him. When he got to Bill's suite he suggested to the others that he read some poetry in Brian's memory just before the band played.

Over in the park things had got under way with the Third Ear Band shortly after 1pm. Their music was the total antithesis of the Stones' and perhaps it was because of the atmosphere, the vibe, that they, somewhat surprisingly, seemed to go down quite well. Next on were King Crimson, who performed their anthemic 'Court of the Crimson King' along with a breakneck speed version of '21st Century Schizoid Man' and 'Mars from Holst's Planet Suite'; for many people they were the highlight of the day – apart from the Stones of course.

The South London band Screw were probably not the right kind of band for such a day, but their relationship with Blackhill won them right of entry; they may well have wished it hadn't. They were called "naive and pretentious" with just a cover of Captain Beefheart's 'Gimme Dat Harp Boy' sounding vaguely good enough. Later, three members of Screw, along with about nine others, were stopped by police and charged with possession of drugs; it must have ruined what had already been a bad day for the band. Brian's old friend Alexis Korner's new drummer-less band, which he called New Church, were a late addition to the bill, but they too failed to sparkle. Despite Korner's gritty vocals and their enthusiastic playing they were under-rehearsed and failed to impress.

Roger Chapman led Family through a rousing set, which in any other circumstances would have been much better received, but the crowd was getting restless for the main attraction. However, their songs, including the excellent 'How-Hi-The-Li' and 'Dim' from their second album, *Family Entertainment*, drew enthusiastic applause from a crowd that was continuing to grow bigger. Whoever followed them was going to find it hard, The Battered Ornaments, without Pete Brown, found it impossible and just could not cut it despite the odd good moment.

While Family were on stage the Stones climbed onboard an old army ambulance at the Londonderry House to make their way past Buckingham Palace and on into Hyde Park. The Angels and greasers cleared a path as they made their way slowly to the backstage area.

"Family were as always good, harder on stage than on record. Veins standing out on his neck Roger Chapman whipped himself into towel-flaying & mike-bashing passion – a bit cruel to the mikes who were appearing free as well." – New Musical Express

• Opposite – *King Crimson on stage*

• Next Page – *The Stones arrive backstage in the converted ambulance*

"The massive stage decorated with plastic palm trees was fast filling up, with people hanging from the scaffolding of the two flanking supports." – New Musical Express

The backstage area was a cross between a scrum and a zoo. There were hundreds of people crushed into an area that would have never been allowed in our modern-day health and safety obsessed society. In fact, not much that happened at Hyde Park would have passed muster by the standards of today; not least the stage and the huge numbers of people who were beginning to congregate on it in order to get as close as possible to the action.

Shortly after 4.30pm the Stones bundled off the dark green ambulance. First came Keith, then Mick, clutching his poetry book and dressed in the outfit he had worn to the White Ball two days earlier; he had intended to wear a snakeskin suit, designed by Ossie Clark, but since it was one of the hottest days of the year he switched at the last minute. In contrast to Mick, Charlie wore a lime-green granddad vest and a pair of rather ordinary looking trousers. The band went straight into a caravan, to which the head of security for the day, Klein, had cleared a path; the caravan looked as if it had been liberated from a slightly down-at-heel campsite. Once inside they had a short rehearsal of their opening number, a song they had never played on stage before, nor even recorded, which gives some idea of their confidence. Appropriately, given their heritage, Brian's original concept for the band and Mick Taylor's pedigree, it was to be a blues tune. They also had to tune up, which they did using a harmonica – a challenge in any circumstances but with the noise going on all around them it proved especially difficult. There were faces pressed at every window, everyone eager to catch a glimpse of

the Stones in private, as though they were getting some extra special insight into their strange world; Charlie passed apples out of the window of the caravan to the voyeurs.

Mick was anxious to establish exactly what was going to happen when the band went on stage. Having told the others that he was to read some poetry he began asking around as to who was doing the introductions. Enter 26-year-old Sam Cutler, who was working for Blackhill and running the on stage announcements and introductions. Mick explained that he was going to read a piece of Shelley's poetry before the band played, but he needed some quiet. "I'm goin' to read this for Brian and I hope they all agree with what I say about him." As he finished explaining what he needed Sam dropped what must have been a bombshell for Mick and the others. "I reckon there's 650,000 people out there." "No!" Was all that Mick could reply. A little earlier Cutler had told the crowd that he thought they were maybe 250,000 to 300,000 strong – three times the size of a Wembley cup final crowd.

"Blackhill told us the Stones would appear and urged us to provide 1,500 watts or more. On the day we could only muster 600 watts, so we asked the groups to loan us their gear and the roadies responded magnificently. They humped our two and a half tons and 1,500 watts of equipment into the towers quickly and efficiently. People scrambling about the stage kicked the whole mains feed out on three occasions." – Charlie Watkins

"Brian will be at the concert; it will depend on what you believe in. If you're an agnostic then he's dead and that's it. I want to make it that Brian's send-off from the world is filled with as much happiness as possible." – Mick

The crowd that had gathered was not 650,000. Ever since the event there was doubt about the real figure, which was probably closer to 250,000, but as it was free nobody counted accurately, nor cared. It was certainly the largest crowd ever to assemble in Britain for a concert; it was said that not since the death of Rudolph Valentino had such a large group of people got together to idolise an artist or person. The myth of half a million fans was perpetuated by a TV programme that suggested this figure.

Whatever the numbers, from the stage the crowd looked like a sea of different colours. The event had attracted not just Stones' fans but weirdos, the agit prop theatre, happy clappy Christians, hippies, skinheads, as well as almost every other kind of head. It had also attracted a big crowd of friends of the band and pop royalty. Paul and Linda McCartney, who had married three months earlier, were there, along with Eric Clapton and his girlfriend Alice Ormsby-Gore; fellow Blind Faith member Ginger Baker took his daughter. Donovan, who had performed at the Blind Faith free concert, was there too. Other musicians included Chris Barber, whose band Brian had gone to see at Cheltenham Town Hall when Alexis Korner played a blues

set, Kenny Lynch, at least one of the Hollies, photographer Michael Cooper, singer Julie Felix, Mama Cass and Marsha Hunt who had recently begun a solo career after appearing in the stage musical *Hair*.

"A man was taken to hospital with blood streaming from his head after a backstage scuffle. Police confiscated several knives and made 12 arrests. Ambulancemen were kept busy and dealt with more than 400 casualties, nearly all fainting cases." – The People, 6 July 1969

• Opposite – *Marianne Faithfull climbs the steps to the main stage just before the Stones go on*   • Above – *Chris Barber and his Jazz Band*
• Page 118 – *Marianne with her son Nicholas*
• Page 119 – *The Stones make their way to the stage*

"The greatest rock 'n' roll band in the world. They're incredible; let's hear it for the Stones!" – Sam Cutler at 5.25pm, Saturday 5 July 1969

•Opposite – *Sam Cutler*

"*Alright! Ok now listen, will you just cool it for a minute 'cos I really would like to say sommit for Brian. I'd really dig it if you would be with us while I do it. I really don't know how to do this kind of thing, but I'm goin' to try. I'd like to say a few words that I feel about Brian and I'm sure you do and what we feel about him just going when we didn't expect him to... Ah you going to be quiet or not? I'm going to say something written by Shelley.*"
– Mick

Peace, peace! he is not dead, he doth not sleep –
He hath awakened from the dream of life –
'Tis we, who lost in stormy visions, keep
With phantoms an unprofitable strife,
And in mad trance, strike with our spirit's knife
Invulnerable nothings. – We decay
Like corpses in a charnel; fear and grief
Convulse us and consume us day by day,
And cold hopes swarm like worms within our living clay.

The One remains, the many change and pass;
Heaven's light forever shines, Earth's shadows fly;
Life, like a dome of many-coloured glass,
Stains the white radiance of Eternity,
Until Death tramples it to fragments. – Die,
If thou wouldst be with that which thou dost seek!
Follow where all is fled!

Adonais by Percy Bysshe Shelley (1792–1822)

• Opposite – *Mick reads Shelley*

• Next Page – *Tom Keylock releasing the butterflies. 3,000 were supplied by Brian Gardiner, who bred them as a hobby. A number were sterilised, but others were not. A further 500 came from World Wide Butterflies; they were all unsterilised. They cost £300*

Set list

I'm Yours and I'm Hers

Jumpin' Jack Flash

(Mercy Mercy)

Stray Cat Blues

No Expectations

I'm Free

Down Home Girl

Love In Vain

Loving Cup

Honky Tonk Women

Midnight Rambler

(I Can't Get No) Satisfaction

Street Fighting Man

Sympathy For The Devil

"99% of the audience came to listen and not (as they might have done five years ago) to scream."

– Disc,
12 July 1969

The set from the Stones was longer than they had ever played before, and very different from what their audiences of old would have been expecting. But with two years absence from the stage and several new releases behind them it was bound to be much altered from the days of the package tours and even the 30-minute sets that they were playing on the 1967 tour.

Perhaps the most surprising song of all was their opener, 'I'm Yours and I'm Hers' – it wasn't even a Stones song. Written by Texan albino blues guitarist Johnny Winter, it featured on his debut Columbia album that had been out only for a month. Keith had bought it back in June and it was his suggestion that they opened the show with it. It was the one and only time the band has ever performed it on stage.

Next up was another first, the first time the Stones ever performed 'Jumpin' Jack Flash' on stage, although at least it was very familiar to the crowd, having topped the charts for a couple of weeks the previous summer. On their tour of the US in the autumn it became their usual opener, getting their set off to the kind of high-energy start that was needed. Don Covay's 'Mercy Mercy' was another less than obvious choice given that it was recorded way back in May 1965 and showed up on the *Out of Our Heads* album. Neither 'Stray Cat Blues' nor 'No Expectations' had ever been performed live before, having first appeared on *Beggars Banquet*.

Another first live performance was 'I'm Free', a track from *Out of Our Heads*. 'Down Home Girl' was the oldest number in their set, having been recorded in late 1964 and released on the band's second British album. From an old song they moved to a very old song, a cover of Robert Johnson's 'Love in Vain' which he had recorded in 1937. However, it was a new song for the band as they had only recorded it a few months earlier; it appeared on *Let it Bleed* which became the band's 10th British and 14th American album when it came out at the end of 1969.

•Page 131 – *Mick sings 'I'm Yours, I'm Hers'*

'Loving Cup' was another new Mick and Keith song, which they had been working on in the studio; it finally made it onto *Exile on Main Street* in 1972. They followed 'Honky Tonk Women', their new single, with 'Midnight Rambler', which became the opening track of side 2 of *Let it Bleed*; in some press it was referred to as "The Boston Gambler".

'Satisfaction' was the only survivor from the Stones' last tour in April 1967; strangely, their performance, of what was even then classic Stones, was ragged and out of tune, none of which stopped almost the entire crowd rising to their feet in salute. 'Street Fighting Man' from *Beggars Banquet* preceded 'Sympathy For The Devil', both of which were from *Beggars Banquet*. For their closing number the Stones were joined on stage by Ginger Johnson's African Drummers; Johnson was a veteran of the London jazz club scene.

"We're gonna do a song off our new album that'll be released in about 10 years' time. It's called 'I just want a drink from my lovin' cup'."
– Mick

"This is an historic occasion and the press of the world are here. This is the crucial concert for the whole pop music scene in London." – Sam Cutler

Sam Cutler's introduction of 'the Greatest Rock 'n' Roll Band in the World' was spontaneous and has become entirely appropriate and synonymous ever since. Cutler used it to introduce them throughout their US tour later in the year and it can be heard on *Get Your Ya Yas Out*, their live album recorded on the tour. On *Ya Yas* they very definitely lived up to their billing, but at Hyde Park it was a very different story. They were as much the blues band that Brian wanted them to be as a rock 'n' roll band – Mick just hoped people wouldn't think they were back in July 1962.

No matter how great the Stones have always been on stage it was a huge ask for them to come back after such a long lay-off, and with Mick Taylor, who was barely broken in, and expect them to perform at their best. Indeed, the choice of material was, in part, their undoing. Never again have they ignored their early hits in such cavalier fashion. By the opening date on the US tour at Fort Collins, Colorado, in November they had reinstated 'Under My Thumb' and added 'Carol' and 'Little Queenie' – two out and out rock 'n' roll songs from Chuck Berry, one of Mick and Keith's earliest inspirations. The new material, especially the songs from *Let It Bleed*, were also featured on the US tour, but by then they had been honed to perfection.

Engineer Ray Pickett who did a great job in supplying the soundtrack for the TV show captured the band's performance in the park on the eight-track Pye Mobile Studio. However, it was one of the first concerts that was recorded, warts 'n' all; previous Stones' live performances had been heavily overdubbed in the studio and in some cases had not even be recorded live – screams were simply added to studio recordings to give the effect of an in-concert recording.

But did it matter that the Stones in the Park were ragged? Not for those who were there. It's the same with so many live recordings: take away the ambience, the atmosphere and the visual stimulus and you can often have a sound that seems to be nothing like what your mind recalls.

"It was a nostalgic, out-of-tune ritual that summed up a decade of pop." – Chris Welch, *Melody Maker* 12 July 1969

•Above – *Chuck Berry*

As the people drifted away from the park there were the regular London newspaper sellers offering the evening papers. On the placards beside their stalls in big bold letters was "Mick Jagger Cited in Divorce Suit". This was 22-year-old Marianne's divorce from her husband, 25-year-old John Dunbar, who was also the father of her son, Nicholas. Marianne's life was full to overflowing. On Saturday evening she and Mick went to see Chuck Berry and The Who at the Royal Albert Hall – he probably played 'Little Queenie' and 'Carol', while The Who stuck to 'Tommy'.

For so many people it is one of their special memories of a decade in which Britain showed the world that pop could be more than just pap, when pop found a voice beyond the singles charts and the pages of the weekly teen magazines. According to Paul Conroy, who would later run Virgin Records, it was all so very relaxed. "I was the Social Secretary at Ewell Technical College in Surrey. Family was my favourite group so it was a must for me to go. I went with Chris Briggs and a friend of mine called Chris Jenvey; both of them went to Ewell Tech. Also with us was a girl called Jane who, at the time, was seeing Greg Lake of King Crimson. They'd played their second ever gig at Ewell the previous April for the sum of £15. We drove up from Purley in Chris Jenvey's mum's car which was an open-top Triumph."

It was the gig of the summer and the fact that it was a lovely day, as well as being free, brought people together in larger numbers than ever before. Did Brian's death add to the numbers? It's impossible to say, but it certainly created a mood for the day that was for some in the audience very special. Many fans would later claim that they saw a ghostly apparition of Brian on stage – this was in fact nothing more than a huge photograph of the former Stone on the back wall of the stage, which could be viewed over Mick's right shoulder. As one newspaper said the day after the concert, "Love 'em or loath 'em, the Stones are still the Pied Pipers of Britain's youth." That was very much the essence of the concert; it was a very special day at which people saw possibilities beyond the restrictions of pop. In the future, perhaps, everything was possible.

The following week in the pop press there was even mention of The Beatles playing a one-off show, possibly in Hyde Park. We all know they didn't so the question "Were you at the Hyde Park concert?" can only ever mean the Rolling Stones... the Greatest Rock 'n' Roll Band in the World.

"The Rolling Stones would never be the same. The band changed, but the band went on – drawing strength from our troubles, taking risks, leading the way and always the Stones..."

– Bill Wyman in *Stone Alone*

The Dream is Over

Brian Jones was the first icon of his generation to pass away; it was not long before others of his generation would follow. For music fans around the world he was the first of their stars to be lost. Of course, Buddy Holly had died, as had Eddie Cochran, but they were both from another era, an older generation who just didn't get it. Everyone expected them to be like shooting stars that arrived and then faded almost as quickly as they appeared. Pop did not last, its stars went on to become something more respectable – some became film stars, while others got married and got a proper job.

"I don't think he had enough love or understanding."
– George Harrison

Following the Hyde Park concert it was announced that Brian's funeral was to take place on Thursday 10 July. On the morning of the funeral Bill and his girlfriend went to Brian's parents' home in Cheltenham for what he described as an "intensely emotional meeting". During the morning Charlie and Shirley Watts, Stu and his wife along with Tom Keylock all arrived at Brian's former home. Everywhere there were flowers and wreaths including an 8ft high floral arrangement of red and yellow roses from the Stones.

The funeral cortège of 14 cars, 4 of which contained flowers, made its way to Cheltenham Parish Church; as a schoolboy this was where Brian had been confirmed and sung in the choir. As the cars slowly made their way through the streets of Cheltenham hundreds of people stood to pay their respects in the gently falling rain; many wept openly. For Brian the sky was crying.

At the church well over 500 people had gathered to say goodbye. Among them was the band's former manager, Eric Easton, but no Andrew Loog Oldham. Also there was Suki Potier, while his old girlfriend Linda Lawrence and Brian's son Julian, had flown in from America. Mick and Marianne were not there, having gone to Australia, where Mick was to begin filming. There was no sign of Keith and Anita, neither did Allen Klein show up, nor did many of Brian's other, so-called, friends.

There was not enough room inside the large church for everyone, so fans gathered in the churchyard as the casket was carried inside. The service was simple, taking

"He was like a man hanging on to a live wire – it hurt but he couldn't let go."
– Linda Lawrence

just 15 minutes. Canon Hopkins in his address spoke of Brian "the rebel", which Bill, in particular, thought a little cynical, but it showed the difficulty of the older generation in understanding Brian's generation – something that he grappled with all his life. "I hold in my hand a telegram which Mr and Mrs Jones treasure more than they can say. It was sent to them by Brian some little while ago after he had come into conflict with the law. The telegram said 'Please don't worry. Don't jump to hasty conclusions and please don't judge me too harshly'." However there's no denying Brian left a trail of damage, but he also left a legacy of some great music.

When the service at the church was over Brian's coffin was driven the 3 miles to Prestbury Cemetery. Once again hundreds lined the route as well as filling the cemetery. Here the two hundredweight solid bronze casket, which had been specially flown over from New York, was lowered into the freshly dug grave; many of the mourners threw a single red rose on top of the coffin. Press photographers anxious to get their pictures were not always as respectful as they should have been, and Brian's mother was jostled as she held young Julian close to her.

Afterwards Brian's family and those from the Stones' family went back to Brian's parents' home for what must have been a difficult time for everyone.

"We had our violent disagreements, but we never stopped loving him." – Lewis Jones

• Opposite – *The Stones 8ft high floral tribute*

• Next page – *Frank Thorogood on the far right, with Astrid, Bill & Charlie*

Outlaw Blues

It was in May '69 that Mick agreed to take on the role of notorious Australian outlaw; it was a time when everything and anything in the Stones' world was far from certain. Brian's position in the group, though precarious because of the problems over whether or not he would be allowed into the USA, was still unresolved. For Mick the film may have been something of a potential career move away from the Stones. For years singers had naturally gravitated towards the cinema to further their careers, and Mick was no different, having already worked on *Performance* with Anita Pallenberg.

"Huh! Those Australians. They really are dummies! But you can bet that there will probably be one or two people protesting when I get there – and I'll throw beer at them. They're so pathetic!" – Mick, July 1969

As Britain woke up to Sunday newspaper reports of the Stones in the Park, Mick and Marianne were busy packing as they were about to fly to Australia in the afternoon. Accompanied by one of the Stones' security people they made an overnight stop in Los Angeles and flew on to Sydney on Monday evening, arriving the following morning to a less than enthusiastic Australian press corps. Maybe Mick's interview with *Disc* in which he called Australians "pathetic" had got there ahead of him?

As Mick and Marianne were waking up in Los Angeles the Sussex coroner in East Grinstead was passing the 'misadventure' verdict on Brian's death, while plans for his funeral were being finalized. In the same week Bill Wyman was also in court seeking a divorce from the mother of his son; they had married in 1959 on Bill's 23rd birthday. They, like many other 'pop couples', found that the music

"When it comes to acting, they make out it's something special. It's not. It's just as natural as singing. You can either do it – or you can't." – Mick, July 1969

"It's very masculine and we've sold several. They cost 85 guineas each." – Michael Fish's business partner

business and marriage did not mix too well; especially when fame came after a wedding. Brian's former chauffeur was busy cashing in on his former boss's death by selling his 'exclusive' story of the drugs and the women to a Sunday newspaper; it was all very seedy, but also very predictable.

Anna Wohlin, who stayed with Bill and his Swedish girlfriend in the days after Brian's death and the Hyde Park concert, took a flight back home to Sweden as soon as the inquest was over. Nothing more was heard from her until she, like others, had things to say about what happened at Cotchford Farm that didn't jive with what she had told the police when they interviewed her on the morning after the drowning.

Mick, perhaps getting into character for his role as Ned Kelly, acted tough in an interview just before he left for the filming; he had several uncomplimentary things to say about Australians, but he also revealed that he was getting fed up with Britain. "I'm getting out of England. I want some peace and quiet. So Marianne and I are going to live in Ireland. England has got too over-populated." The projected move may also have been for tax reasons, which would come to a head over the next couple of years, resulting in the whole band moving to France in March 1971.

The press in Britain were still getting to grips with Mick wearing the dress at Hyde Park, although it certainly seemed to do Michael Fish's business no harm – he reported some good sales, including three to Sammy Davis Jr, one in black, one in brown and one in champagne. The press was anxious to see how Australia would react to Mick, especially if he wore a dress down under.

"My first numbing impression when I saw him was 'This isn't Mick Jagger, it's Barry Humphries having us on'." – Peter Bowers, *Sydney Sun*

Mick must have had an inkling of what he was going to face in Australia given his comments to the British press. There had been the petitions; there had been hundreds of column inches given over to his appearance as Ned Kelly and endless radio phone-in programmes attacking the audacity of the film company for casting Mick in the role. One cartoon summed it all up by saying, "I'd Slip Into Yer Armour Smartly, Ned, Mate," while the *Sydney Daily Mirror* lampooned him with a cartoon questioning his love of cross-dressing: "This is the scene where you smash 20 sheriffs to the ground with your handbag."

With one gang threatening to kidnap Mick and cut his hair, security at the airport was tight and also as Mick and Marianne made their way to the Chevron Hotel in the King's Cross area of Sydney. There were a few days set aside for Mick and Marianne to recover from their long flight before shooting was to begin. The film, written by Ian Jones and Tony Richardson, who was also the director, was based upon the life of the notorious 19th-century outlaw who has been called Australia's Robin Hood. Richardson's credits had included *Look Back in Anger* and *A Taste of Honey*; he was very much an "English theatrical style" movie director, which made it strange for him to be making such a film.

Marianne was cast as Ned's sister, Maggie, and besides Mick being the butt of most Australians' wrath at the casting there were also complaints that the film was to take place in New South Wales rather than Victoria, which is where Kelly had operated. The British production company had decided to film around the small town of Braidwood, 125 miles southwest of Sydney. Most of the cast was Australian though, with the notable exception of Mark McManus, a Scottish actor who had moved to Australia during the 1960s and appeared in *Skippy the Bush Kangaroo*.

According to Marianne, "Tony Richardson talked Mick into doing *Ned Kelly* and I wanted to go because I'd been working three months in *Hamlet*, and Mick was always going on holiday with Keith and Anita without me, and I felt very left out." It was a move that was to prove fatal for their relationship, and to leave scars on Marianne that took decades to even partially heal.

"Mick was wearing a maroon maxi-length coat, black and white checked flared trousers, a white Isadora scarf, a straw hat, black field boots, and an Italian leather fringe purse over his shoulder." – Bill Wyman in *Rolling with the Stones*

Daily Mirror

5d. Thursday, August 7, 1969 · · · · No. 20,408

1052

'We have nothing fresh to put to the men'

SHOCK FOR STEEL STRIKERS: NO UNION BACKING

By BRYN JONES and KENELM JENOUR

UNION leaders will NOT declare the South Wales steel dispute official when they meet the 1,300 blastfurnacemen strikers today.

This shock for the unofficial strikers was disclosed at Port Talbot last night by Blastfurnacemen's Union district secretary Hector Smith.

The strikers, whose stoppage has led to a total shutdown at the huge Abbey and Margam steel-making plant, had firmly expected their leaders to make it official—and announce the fact at a mass meeting today.

But Mr. Smith, after a day of talks with union general secretary Jim Barry, said last night:

"There is nothing new, nothing fresh, that we have to put to the men. We simply hope to convince them that they should go back to work."

At today's meeting, Mr. Barry and other leaders of his union are bound to get a stormy reception.

The blow to the strikers' hopes came as Employment Minister Mrs. Barbara Castle waited in London for a message from Mr. Barry.

Message

Mrs. Castle's expected announcement of a court of inquiry into the dispute depended on getting an assurance from Mr. Barry that it would help to improve the chances of persuading the men to go back.

Late last night it was believed that Mr. Barry had asked Mrs. Castle to hold up the announcement till after today's mass meeting.

The employers' spokes-

Barbara is urged to set up inquiry

man—British Steel Corporation Personnel and Social Policy Director Ron Smith—had urged Mrs. Castle to order the inquiry.

Mr. Smith headed a team of three who travelled by private plane and car from Wales to London to meet the Minister.

Mrs. Castle is understood to have agreed. But the announcement — naming the man to head the inquiry—had to wait for that "green light" call from the Blastfurnacemen's Mr. Barry.

Officials were puzzled that Mr. Barry had not contacted the Ministry until midday yesterday.

By then, it was too late for him to travel to London and join Trades Union Congress acting general secretary Victor Feather for last-minute talks.

The Steel Corporation's chairman Lord Melchett, broke off his Majorca holiday yesterday and flew back to London because of the strike.

The blastfurnacemen's strike began six weeks ago. They stopped work in support of a claim for a £1-a-week pay rise for about 140 low-paid workers.

The employers say they will not negotiate while the strike is on.

An inquest on Mary Jo 'within two months'

From TONY DELANO in New York

AN inquest on Mary Jo Kopechne, the 28-year-old blonde who died in Senator Edward Kennedy's car, now seems a strong possibility.

Although a judge refused yesterday to allow a plea for the inquest, his decision was over a technicality. District Attorney Edmund Dinis, who made the plea, was confident that the inquest would be held within two months.

District court judge James Boyle of Martha's Vineyard, Massachusetts, where Kennedy's car drove off a bridge last month, did not rule out an inquest.

The judge told Dinis that his request was "unclear" and called for more information.

Dinis described the judge's reply as "satisfactory" and his office indicated that a new application would now be made.

The district attorney said: "I expect the inquest to be held, and that all pertinent witnesses will be called."

These would be certain to include the other guests of the party which Kennedy and Mary Jo attended before the death crash.

Request

Dinis also said that he expected a post-mortem examination of Mary Jo's body would be carried out.

A doctor decided at the time of her death that an autopsy was unnecessary.

A request by Dinis for an inquest had already been turned down by a Superior Court judge because he did not consider himself competent to order it.

But Dinis—upset by criticism that he had not probed the accident thoroughly enough — then went to the District Court.

Judge Boyle, as the district judge, should hold the inquest himself.

But this is complicated by Boyle being the man who gave Kennedy a suspended two-month jail sentence for leaving the scene of the accident.

His part in the earlier case might disqualify him from holding the inquest.

Kennedy has said that he is prepared to co-operate in any way if an inquest is held.

What the Mirror Says.—
See Page Two

MARIANNE FLIES OFF TO MICK

THE difficult weeks in hospital are over. Now Marianne Faithfull is free to recuperate, relax . . . and take up her life again.

Still pale and rather nervous, she sits in a car and smokes a cigarette just before driving away from Mount St. Margaret Hospital in Sydney, Australia.

Next stop: The airport—and a flight to her boy friend, Mick

Jagger of the Rolling Stones.

Before setting off yesterday, 22-year-old Marianne spoke hesitantly about her collapse at a Sydney hotel after a drugs overdose . . . and of the doctors and nurses who cared for her.

"I was virtually dead," she said. "They saved my life.

"I expect it will be at least two months before I recover fully."

Marianne, who wore a mauve mini-skirt, a blazer with pink and mauve stripes and pink calf-length boots, added: "I will spend a week riding horses, relaxing and watching Mick on the set of his film."

Mick, 25, is playing the legendary Australian bushranger Ned Kelly in a film being shot near Canberra.

The role of Ned Kelly's sister was to have been played by Marianne. But she was replaced after she collapsed a day after arriving in Australia with Mick early last month.

With Marianne yesterday was her mother, Baroness Erisso. She said that she and her daughter would spend a week with Mick—and then they would both return to Britain.

"Brian had just died too. I can't remember very much about it, and then there was the concert in Hyde Park and these were the things that brought me down. Especially Brian dying. I don't really remember what happened." – Marianne, in 1974

On the morning of Wednesday 9 July Mick sat in his suite at the Chevron Hotel giving an interview, which was proving to be difficult as Marianne, who was in their bedroom, kept interrupting his smooth flow by calling out to him. Suddenly, at around 11.30, she staggered into the room, cried out and collapsed on the floor. According to Marianne, "This was really the beginning of the mess. When I got there, I took 150 sleepers and that's the beginning of my unreliability." Marianne was unconscious: a frightened Mick immediately called down to reception and an ambulance was soon there to take Marianne to St Vincent's hospital.

Mick followed the ambulance in a taxi and Marianne was taken straight into casualty and put on a saline drip. She was in a coma, and things were critical. Soon afterwards the New South Wales police arrived, eager to investigate the causes of her collapse but they were told by the hospital that her condition was so serious that she could see no one. Naturally they were quickly followed by the press, who camped out at the hospital to report on whatever happened next. Mick gave a press conference in which he accused Australians of being even more puritanical then other "colonial nations such as South Africa". Mick's diplomatic skills were a little off, but he was also very worried.

When Mick returned to the hotel the police were there to interview him and to search his suite; they eventually left carrying away several containers and a number of capsules. There was no suggestion that Mick was in any way implicated, but the police seemed fairly certain that Marianne had not just taken sleeping pills.

The following morning, with Marianne in hospital and unable to see anyone, Mick flew to Melbourne to film Ned Kelly's hanging scene at the jail. It's the one where he looks at the camera and utters Kelly's last words, "Such is life." After he had finished filming in Melbourne he flew straight back to Sydney to see Marianne in hospital, by which time she was out of danger. Marianne's Austrian-born mother, Baroness Erisso, flew to Sydney from London to be with her daughter, while Mick continued filming, although for a few days a virus hit the cast and everything ground to a halt.

On 27 July, the day after his 26th birthday, Mick went back to Sydney to spend the afternoon at the hospital with Marianne. They wandered around the grounds of Mount St Margaret's Hospital in Ryde, a Sydney suburb where Marianne had been moved in order to recuperate. On 6 August Marianne was discharged from hospital; wearing a mauve mini-skirt and blazer she was taken to the airport where she flew to Canberra to join Mick, who was filming not far from the Australian capital. They spent a week together before Marianne flew to Switzerland with her mother to convalesce at a sanatorium in Kreuzlingen.

"Marianne turns me on to lots of good things. She has led me into music, drama and literature, which I haven't read before. I turn her on to things more basic. I don't think she's taken an overdose of drugs." – Mick

•Page 184/185 – *Mick talks with director Tony Richardson*

"I know people may have thought me crazy and I had great difficulty at first in getting a studio to back my judgement. But the moment I met Mick I knew he was perfect for the role." – Tony Richardson, August 1969

Because Marianne was not needed for filming the early scenes in *Ned Kelly* there was initially no concern about her being in hospital and missing from the set. However, it quickly became apparent that she was in no fit state to work, and so Tony Richardson began hunting round for a replacement. 'Big T' as Richardson was known on set, chose a 20-year-old drama student named Diane Craig to play Mick's sister; born in Northern Ireland, she would go on to appear in numerous television programmes.

In the middle of August Mick was on location near Canberra filming a scene about the siege of Glenrowan. While he was holding a replica revolver it backfired and a piece of metal embedded itself in his hand. Bleeding from the cut he was driven the 30 miles to hospital in Canberra, where he was stitched up and told to rest for three days. With time on his hands Mick did an interview in which he once again managed to upset some of the more sensitive souls in Australia by announcing. "I think we're all latent homosexuals. Like most men, Ned Kelly probably had affairs with women. And he had a great camaraderie with men."

With filming all wrapped up at the end of the first week of September Mick flew home from Australia, his work finished on a movie that was to be far from popular with either the critics or the public. Arguably, if Mick hadn't appeared in the film it may well have sunk without trace.

"Jagger's best film role to date is still in Godard's One Plus One, where he can be seen doing what he does best: just singing." – Time magazine, August 1970

Back home, work had been continuing on the Stones' new album, while 'Honky Tonk Women' had topped the charts for five weeks in the UK and four weeks in America – musically things were well and truly back on track. Ten days before Mick arrived home Granada aired their 53-minute film *The Stones in the Park* at 10.30pm on Tuesday 2 September. With an edit that jumped around, failing to show the whole set or the set in the order in which it was played, it failed to meet with universal approval – but can anything filmed in such a way ever live up to the reality?

As the old saying goes... you had to be there.

LONDON ITV

1.45-4.0 RACING FROM EPSOM. 2.0, 2.30, 3.5, 3.40 races.
4.15—NEWS; PAULUS.
4.30—CROSSROADS.
4.55—PAPER BAG PLAYERS. With Judith Martin, Irving Burton, Betty Osgood, Donald Ashwander, Charles Leipart.
5.20—MAGPIE. With Susan Stranks, Tony Bastable, Pete Brady.
5.50—NEWS.
6.3—TODAY. With Eamonn Andrews.
6.30—TUESDAY FILM: Silver River (Western 1948). Starring Errol Flynn, Ann Sheridan. A riverboat gambler becomes one of the leading lights of Silver City.
8.30—BEST THINGS IN LIFE. Starring Harry Corbett, June Whitfield. A day-trip to France means romance for Mabel . . . or so she thinks.
9.0—WHO-DUN-IT: The Eyes of the Buddha. The police are faced with a puzzling murder—a killing in a pagoda.
10.0—NEWS AT TEN.
10.30—STONES IN THE PARK. The Rolling Stones and their pop concert in Hyde Park.
11.30—THE ACTOR AND THE ROLE. Irene Worth as Celia Coplestone from Cocktail Party.
12.0—ONE OFF. Fred Dinenage talks to Rev Whitlock, author and Agricultural consultant to the Methodist Missionary Society.

The Greatest Rock 'n' Roll Band in the World

At every gig on their US tour Sam Cutler introduced the Stones as "the Greatest Rock 'n' Roll Band in the World". They were, and have remained so ever since. Many have tried to claim the title as theirs, but no one has come close. With the triumph of Hyde Park behind them the band sensed a renaissance, and as the tour across America unfolded their position seemed secure. But by the time they got to Altamont the naivety and the ambition combined to create a disaster that for most people showed the dream was over. The sixties had drawn to a close in every sense.

"What made us decide to get back into it was Hyde Park. It was such a unique feeling." – Keith, October 1969

Two days after Mick flew home from Australia the band's manager, Allen Klein, announced that the band would begin their 6th US tour on 26 October, giving them a little over six weeks to get everything together. It was an ambitious target. But with work largely completed on the new album that Keith had decided should be called *Let it Bleed*, another greatest hits album just released in both America and Britain, everything was ready for the Stones to start once again earning the kind of money everyone imagined they always had done. A month after Mick got back a telex was sent from the Stones' office in London to Klein, pleading for cash. "We still have no money. What has gone wrong over there? How does one keep the wolves from the door? Please reply as this is really desperate."

On a more mundane level, Mick and Marianne's drug case was once again postponed because of the pending US tour; Mick grabbed the opportunity for a two-week holiday in Indonesia while preparations continued for the band's first US tour in three years and their most ambitious to date.

On Friday 17 October the band met up at London Airport to fly to Los Angeles. On arrival Mick and Keith stayed with Steve Stills in Laurel Canyon, while Charlie and his family, Stu and Glyn Johns were staying at a mansion overlooking Sunset Strip that was formerly owned by the Du Pont family;

"The Stones have succeeded in turning outrage into art. Are they really able to use all that money?" – Robert Hilburn, the *Los Angeles Times*

it was to be the band's headquarters while they were in California. Also on the tour, that was now scheduled to start on 1 November, were B.B.King, Ike and Tina Turner, Chuck Berry and Terry Reid.

Before the tour began Mick and Keith worked on finalising *Let it Bleed*, including Merry Clayton's great vocals on 'Gimme Shelter'. It was certainly very different from the way things are done today – this was barely a month before the album's release, and there was no time for anyone to become bored with it. The band's greatest hits album, *Through The Past Darkly,* featuring a picture of the band, Brian included, on its cover, was sitting at No. 2 on the US album charts, on its way to selling a million copies. For the cash-strapped band this was a godsend.

"Yes, I feel I am a Rolling Stone now. I didn't at first. It wasn't like being part of the group until we did that concert in the park. I've done quite a bit of recording with them now, and I'm playing what I want to play. I don't want to play solos all the time – I like to play songs ... We want to do a tour next, probably a world tour in the autumn." – Mick Taylor

•Opposite – *Keith and Anita with baby Marlon who was born on 10 August 1969; Keith picked them up on 18 August and took home the mother and baby they had named after Marlon Brando*

On Friday 7 November the Stones' 6th US tour kicked off at the State University in Fort Collins Colorado. Tickets for this 17-date, 23-show tour sold out in a matter of a few hours and extra shows in New York and Los Angeles were soon added. Basing themselves either in New York or Los Angeles the Stones flew to the gigs, but the logistics caused major difficulties, with the band often appearing late. On the second night they went on at around 4am for their second show. With ticket prices ranging from $4.50 to as high as $8 in New York the Stones grossed almost $2 million, over two and a half times more than on their last US tour in the

Set chosen from

'Jumpin' Jack Flash'
'Carol'
'Stray Cat Blues'
'Love In Vain'
'Midnight Rambler'
'Sympathy for the Devil'
'Prodigal Son'
'You Got To Move'
'Under My Thumb '
'I'm Free'
'Live With Me'
'Gimme Shelter '
'Little Queenie'
'Satisfaction'
'Honky Tonk Women'
'Street Fighting Man'

"After playing every night for three or four years you miss the road." – Keith

summer of 1966. Midway through the tour, their gig at the Forum in Los Angeles grossed $260,000, beating the record set by the Beatles at Shea Stadium in 1966 by $20,000.

By the last show of the three-week tour the Stones had played to around 300,000 fans, which by today's standards may seem small but 40 years ago people were amazed. After appearing at the International Raceway in West Palm Beach, Florida, the band flew to Alabama to record in the eight-track Muscle Shoals Sound. During their three days there one of the tracks they worked on was 'Brown Sugar', a song Mick wrote while filming *Ned Kelly*.

From Muscle Shoals they flew to San Francisco for what the band, and many others, thought might be a west coast Woodstock – a concert to match the three days of peace and music that had taken place just a month after Hyde Park. Originally the 6 December free concert was to have taken place in Golden Gate Park, but city officials would not agree to that venue. Next Sears Point Raceway in Sonoma County was suggested, but eventually Altamont Raceway, 50 miles east of San Francisco, was decided upon – where the biggest crowd yet had been only 6,500.

An area near the highway was chosen as the best place for the stage, to maximise everyone's view. Some thought a quarter of a million fans would show up, and by midnight about 25,000 were already at the site. It was a little above freezing as Saturday dawned, a day on which little would go right; people were flooding in from every direction,

"It was a disaster right from the start. It went wrong from the moment we left Muscle Shoals." – Stu

"There was no provocation; the Angels started the whole violence thing. During our set I could see a guy from the stage who had a knife and just wanted to stab somebody."– Carlos Santana

eventually numbering half a million. There was a 30-mile traffic jam, not helped by the fact that many people just abandoned their cars – ironically it was one of the few ways in which Altamont was like Woodstock. The fans who gathered around the stage found the Hells Angels acting as security guards – but they were very different from the ones at Hyde Park.

Around 1pm Santana took to the stage around three hours late; almost immediately trouble began when the Hells Angels set upon a guy and beat him up. Not content with this, the Angels attacked a naked couple before smashing a photographer's equipment... and his face.

Midway through their fourth song Santana gave up: the Angels had invaded the stage and taken up residence, along with their crates of beer. Jefferson Airplane's set was disrupted too, but they at least managed to finish. The Stones, who were still in their downtown hotel, witnessed none of this but heard about what was going on. Keith was all for not showing up, but he and the band eventually went, concerned that by not going things could turn even nastier.

As the band arrived by helicopter The Flying Burrito Brothers were about to go on, and as the Stones walked to the backstage area Mick was punched in the mouth. Crosby, Stills, Nash and Young were next, and occupied what little of the stage was left by the Angels. Instead of the Grateful Dead going on after CSNY it was decided that the Stones should appear. Sam Cutler tried to clear the stage but eventually gave up. The Stones began with their by now regular opener of 'Jumpin' Jack Flash', followed by 'Carol', 'Stray Cat Blues', 'Love in Vain' and 'Under My Thumb' – during which another fight started out front of the stage.

It was during 'Under My Thumb' that the Hells Angels killed a fan named Meredith Hunter, and although the Stones were uncertain as to exactly what was happening they knew it was a very bad scene. At one point Keith said, "Either those cats cool it, man, or we don't play. Keep it cool! Hey, if you don't cool it, you ain't gonna hear no music!" An Angel grabbed a mike and shouted "Fuck you!"

As if by rote the Stones carried on, although their next number was their first live performance of 'Brown Sugar', followed by 'Midnight Rambler' and then 'Live With Me'. According to Bill, "everyone was playing their asses off, and Mick was brilliant". 'Gimme Shelter' followed, then 'Little Queenie', and 'Satisfaction'. As their set ended a helicopter pilot went onstage and told the band that his was the last chopper, and he was leaving, with or without them, in 10 minutes. They managed 'Honky Tonk Women' and ended the show with 'Street Fighting Man' before racing to the helicopter. The band and 15 others all scrambled on board, vastly exceeding its legal payload; somehow it made it back to San Francisco.

From then on the greatest rock 'n' roll band in the world just got bigger.

"Why are we fighting? Why are we fighting? We don't want to fight at all. Who wants to fight, who is it? Every other scene has been cool. We gotta stop right now. You know, if we can't there's no point." – Mick

Index

This index is a basic guide and therefore does not contain every detail.

Thanks

Thanks are due to Andy Neill for his help on this book. Richard Evans for his masterful recreation of Robert Johnson's recording session on page 135. Kevin Gardner for his superb design work, Becky Ellis for her excellent proof reading and Elizabeth Stone for her editing skills. A big thank you to everyone at the Mirrorpix Archive, Vito Inglese, Alex Waters, Manjit Sandhu and John Mead. Fergus McKenna and David Scripps at Mirrorpix have also been there all along the way.

And also a special thank you to Bill Wyman for sharing his memories of THE gig in Hyde Park.

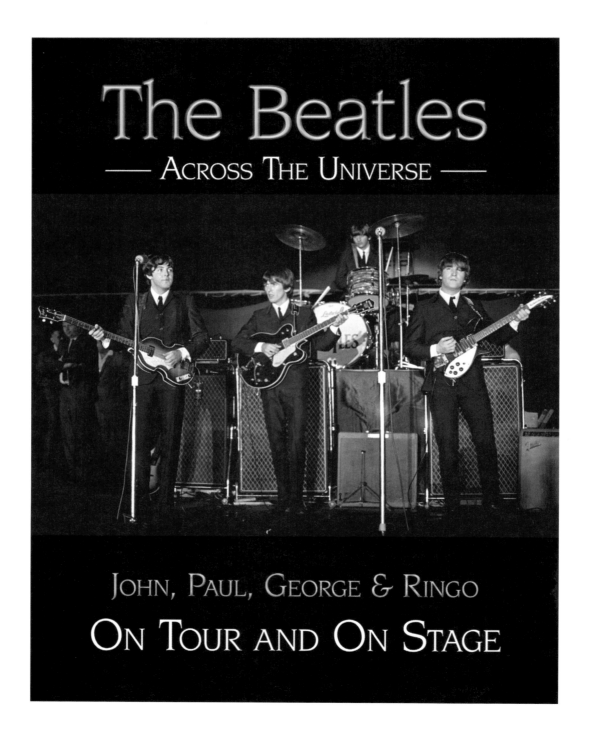

The Beatles

— ACROSS THE UNIVERSE —

JOHN, PAUL, GEORGE & RINGO

ON TOUR AND ON STAGE

Also Available